Date Due			
Jul 10 '50			
IN LIBRARY			
Apr 24 '54			
May 27 '57			
Feb 16 '01			
Aug 23 '61 Pd.			
Oct 11 '61			
May 24 '66			
Mar 16 '67			

AIDS TO HISTORICAL RESEARCH

AIDS TO
HISTORICAL RESEARCH

BY

JOHN MARTIN VINCENT

PROFESSOR EMERITUS OF EUROPEAN HISTORY
JOHNS HOPKINS UNIVERSITY

D. APPLETON–CENTURY COMPANY
INCORPORATED

NEW YORK   LONDON

PREFACE

These pages are offered as a brief review of certain branches of learning which are of first importance in the conduct of historical research in the social sciences. They are primarily intended for the use of beginners in such work. Long experience with graduate students has shown conclusively that an early perspective of the sciences auxiliary to such investigation will lead to a quicker perception of the risks encountered and to sounder habits of research. Experts in these sciences have carried some of them to a high degree of refinement, and it is not expected that every historian will be an expert, but it is his duty to understand the reasoning employed in proof.

The subjects presented are chiefly employed in "external criticism" where the authenticity of a document or its time, place, or source is determined, but some of them are highly important factors in the interpretation of history, and all of them contribute matters of social, economic, or intellectual significance. This work attempts a fresh consideration in the light of later attainments and modern usage.

The many sources from which the text has been gathered are plainly evident, and to those who have given me personal assistance I extend my hearty gratitude.

JOHN MARTIN VINCENT

Johns Hopkins University

CONTENTS

AIDS TO HISTORICAL RESEARCH

I

DEFINITION OF HISTORY

In this age of extensive historical studies a definition of the term *history* may seem to be superfluous. Not only in the traditional fields of national and political development but also in every branch of learning from anthropology to zoölogy an industrious body of students is searching out the origins and progress of sciences as well as peoples. At the same time a clarification of the objects and the relative importance of such investigations is highly important, for the selection of materials and the form of presentation depend upon a proper definition of history.

Without going back to the primitive ages of oral anecdote and minstrelsy, but starting with the first written histories, there has been a slow but positive change in the conception of this art. The Greek word *historia* means "a searching to find out" and would apply just as well to any doctor's thesis of to-day as to history itself; but the contents of the word, the notion of what we are to find out, has experienced a wide extension. Only in one respect has the conception of history remained steadfast: it has to do with mankind. Even the histories of sciences are concerned with the men who discovered and developed them, but when it comes to what we ought to know or write about peoples or nations the answer is far different from what it was in the days of Herodotus, or Thucydides, or Froissart, or even David Hume.

To the first writers of history the object was to preserve the memory of the heroic deeds of men, and these were for the most part performed in battle. Hence the stories of wars to the glorification of nations as well as heroes, from which we gain incidental glimpses of the growth or eclipse of political units. In the fighting era of the middle ages history-writing declined, but the chronicles continued the same course until the art once more emerged in the stories of the crusades and the military-athletic reports of Froissart. Even when more mature accounts of national history appear and statecraft and diplomacy emerge as subjects of interest, war and conflict still occupy great proportions of attention. Not only in warlike ages but in eras of comparative peace down almost to our own day this emphasis on the details of conflict has been prominent in historical writing. Likewise the traditional history contained much about the personal traits and actions of kings and courtiers, the intrigues of nobles and officials, and even the scandals of upper society, this kind of thing no doubt merely satisfying a certain human craving for biographic anecdote.

4

Out of this welter of war and court description there emerge two matters in justification of the writers. First, nations were either solidified or destroyed by wars, and here, with perhaps too much detail, is the story of the process. The growth of modern nations is a most important part of history and the long story of their division or consolidation is in this way in part explained. Second, in the days of absolute sovereigns the fate of peoples was determined by the ambitions, or the whims, or perhaps the indigestions of their rulers; hence the personal character of kings or princes in such cases is a matter for inquiry and explanation. These factors, however, are only two among a multitude of elements which have guided the development of nations or determined the condition of a people at a given moment. Economic, geographic, and other causes were at work and were long overlooked by the writers of history. The prominence of wars and conflicts was due to the worship of the heroic; for ages the profession of arms was regarded as the noblest career of the layman, while honors, rewards, and renown were found on the field of battle.

The changes which have taken place in the conception of history during the twenty-four centuries since Herodotus wrote have been momentous, but slow in coming. During the greater part of this period the military and political story held first place. From time to time writers appeared with a more critical attitude toward their sources, but the theme remained about the same. Although some of the ancients noticed that heat and cold affected peoples, two thousand years passed by before it was seriously asserted that climate and geography influence the life and political conditions of nations, and lines of argument were then used which are no longer acceptable. Political history had one advantage in furnishing a continuous thread upon which the story might be hung, and economic conditions received no extended attention until the eighteenth century. The middle ages regarded the laboring classes as beneath their notice, and only writers on formal law gave any clue to social conditions. Commerce and industry expanded over the known world, but under the sharp criticism of theologians and with no one to connect them with national history.

The isolated instances where economic facts are noted do not relieve the general lack of appreciation of the importance of such data and the consequent unbalanced expositions of national life. At the present day the conception of history is distinctly modern, and the fields of inquiry now considered necessary to its proper understanding have had a rapid expansion during the past two centuries, much accelerated during the past two generations and apparently still increasing.

Mere curiosity, or the desire to entertain, may have led early writers to include in their narratives some description of the social life of the people, but the increase of interest in such details has been steadily parallel to the expansion of democracy. Whatever judgment may be passed on the mutual influence of the two tendencies, it is clear that as fast as ordinary citizens obtained political rights and self-government there followed greater desire to learn about the manners and customs of their predecessors and a consciousness of their part in history.

Historians in the early nineteenth century included some description of the social conditions of their periods, but usually in separate chapters which served as illustrative pictures rather than constructive parts of the narrative. It was scarcely a hundred years ago that Macaulay said, in rebellion against exclusive political and dynastic history, that the true historian "considers no anecdote, no peculiarity of manner, no familiar saying, as too insignificant for his notice, which is not too insignificant to illustrate the operation of laws, of religion and of education, and to mark the progress of the human mind." Even he used his social data too much as literary ornament, but he was headed in a direction which later generations followed with increasing intensity. We have now reached a point where capital and labor are regarded as partners in business, an idea which the middle ages could not have conceived, while we study not only peculiar national habits but the conditions of natural sciences at the time and call in the humani-

7

ties and all branches of modern learning to assist in clarifying our pictures of past conditions.

This does not mean that political history is out of date, for that branch of inquiry must continue to be followed as one phase of human society. It means rather that politics and government cease to cover the story and that other things in the life and experiences of a people are not only essential in themselves but must be employed to explain political movements.

Reasons for writing history have likewise had an evolution of their own and one which is interwoven with the question as to what the contents should be. The primitive object of entertainment was followed by a long period in which instruction and guidance was the purpose, in addition to recording the memorable deeds of the ancestors. This was the motive of Thucydides, and the Roman Dionysius said that history was philosophy teaching by examples, while Machiavelli declared that, since men have always been animated by the same passions, they must look to history for guidance and might even foretell the future by the experiences of their predecessors. The late Professor J. R. Seeley was of the opinion that history should have a practical object, aiming not only to gratify curiosity about the past, but to "modify his views of the present and his forecast of the future."

This was still more the attitude of the earlier

8

writers who made history a series of moral lessons for the guidance of present and future generations, thus entering the domain of prophecy. Quite true, there are moral lessons in the experiences of men and in the conduct of nations, while the consequences of sin and injustice are obvious; but in view of constantly changing conditions there should be caution in forecasting the future. The lives of successful men are full of inspiration which the teacher and the preacher should employ, but they would do well to avoid specific prophecy. The historian may be content to relate what happened.

The same may be said about the histories which were written to show the designs of God in the destinies of peoples. To the authors of these works the plans of Providence were clear and unmistakable, so that a definite design might be traced in the rise and fall of nations. There are still people who see the hand of an angry God in the misfortunes of their neighbors, but this assumes a confidential relationship to the Creator which oversteps the bounds of modesty. With the greatest good-will and reverence one may hesitate to announce or predict the course of Providence.

When history attempts avowedly to teach a lesson, whether moral, political, or theological, there is danger that the facts will in some degree be warped unconsciously to suit the theme, even with the most honorable intentions. Such troubles occur in arguments over historic points when no lesson is involved. What is needed is the exact truth, a matter which was clarified for all time by Lord Bacon when he said, "It is the true office of history to represent the events themselves together with the counsels, and to leave the observations and conclusions thereupon to the liberty and faculty of every man's judgment."

Another definition of history, or rather another object of historical research, is that advocated by the extreme school of sociologists who say that the usual historical narrative is filled with the accidentals of life, while the real aim should be to find the typical elements in human society, regardless of individuals, and eventually determine the "laws of history." Following more or less the methods of biology, they ask the historian to investigate the conditions under which social and political events took place. Taking a given period a certain number of births and deaths will be recorded and at intervals famines and business failures will occur. In seasons of prosperity numerous other kinds of phenomena will be observed, hence it is assumed to be possible to determine the social conditions which *inevitably* precede an agrarian revolt, a religious revival, a burst of excellence in art, or other important movement. In the presentation of such results the individual man, be he king or hero, would either disappear or be used in determining the types of mankind then prevailing.

The criticism that history contains unessential details is in many cases fully justified. Garrulity or lack of perspective will account for much excess baggage; but when this is cast off and we are asked to find a law of recurrence in human events, we are confronted with great stretches of time during which statistics of this kind are inadequate or entirely absent. The compilation of data by indirect means may give some help, but for thousands of years the results remain deficient and unsatisfactory. Types of society and laws must be based on complete information, and the conditions of periods compared must be identical. In the absence of anything like uniformity, laws of recurrence and prediction are at best precarious.

The theory that the history of man has been determined entirely by his environment, by his geographical, geological, and climatic situation, has much to give it support, but few or no writers go to such an extreme. The advocates of economic history usually rest with the view that environment is the most weighty factor in the development of peoples or communities, and they vary in their estimates of the amount of such influences. When stated in unqualified terms, the economic theory fails to take account of intellectual and moral factors which are indispensable to an understanding of human history. It is abundantly evident that human society has been guided by individuals, and at times by great moral and religious motives, and that its intellectual standards must be used as measures of its development. Economic historians give weight to these spiritual elements in varying amounts.

The introduction of environment into historical study had enormous influence in pointing out new channels for investigation. Since this influence began to make itself felt European scholars have produced an increasing volume of works upon economic history, *Volkswirtschaft,* attempting both the development of theories and the description of actual agricultural or commercial practices. Studies of the life and habits of former times have grown also into a science of human geography, in which the mutual relations of mankind and the globe have been formulated. Productions of this kind have been added to the historical materials of every country in the civilized world, and it still remains for the investigator to determine the proportion and weight which these economic factors should have in his particular field of research.

When Macaulay said that no incident or anecdote was insignificant if it illustrated the life of the time, he entered a path that has led men into the great open spaces of research. It may be said that no discovery of science, no change in the methods of industry or agriculture, nor any alteration in the conditions of many things less conspicuous than these is without some weight in historical estimates. Commerce and transportation are no longer local but have become international, and the effects of the change are felt in the remotest hamlet. The story of the transition at any given point is of high importance, and with all these matters looming up the modern scholar is obliged to take account of a mass of factors which his early predecessors ignored.

Certain branches of knowledge relating particularly to humanity have been cultivated to a point where they approach the dignity of sciences. Anthropology, ethnology, and psychology have busied themselves with the primitive qualities, habits, and capacities of mankind with such illuminating results that they must be taken into consideration. The application of these factors in the interpretation of historical movements will be touched upon at various points in these pages.

The modern expansion of historical materials increases the labors of the investigator but does not render a solution of his problems impossible. If one should attempt to write a history of the world from original sources, one lifetime would be insufficient to accomplish the task, but no one does that any more. The few authors who cover such a field in a scholarly manner depend upon the researches of specialists for a large part of their recital, and even the history of one nation requires the help of many minds. Such expansive tasks, except for brief textbooks, are no longer undertaken single-handed. The many volumes of Lingard's *England* or Grote's *History of Greece* have been superseded by the coöperative work of many hands. The *Political History of England* appears in twelve volumes by as many authors; the *Cambridge Modern History* is in twelve large volumes of text in which each chapter has been written by a separate specialist; and in many countries in Europe and in America, when an extensive plan is contemplated, a general editor calls to his aid the men who have given intensive study to the various parts of the field. If a lone author desires to appear in many volumes, he must choose a short period the important events of which may give him an opportunity to cover his chosen field successfully. Gardiner devoted a lifetime of work and fourteen volumes to the half-century which included the Puritan Revolution, and other examples might be cited of limited subjects which have led to extended exposition.

For at least a century historical scholars have realized that the researches of one man must be confined to a limited field if they are to be effective in his lifetime, and this appears everywhere from the minute topics of the doctoral thesis to the seasoned labors of the veteran investigator. Consequently the search for a definition of history is not merely an attempt to put into a few words a theory of human progress or a philosophy of civilization, however important these may be, but a very practical task of establishing a norm by which the historian may measure his small part of the work and select the data which truly exhibit its relative development.

As already noted, the object of history is not primarily to moralize or to predict the future but rather, when contemplating a given period or situation, to inquire and determine how these things came to be. However limited the theme, we are after the truth about its development. We may not start at the known origin of a people or a party and construct a chapter of genesis, but anywhere in the subject we are concerned with growth, development, genetic history.

The early chroniclers had no sense of this, and the theologians held an inverted view of the story of the human race which taught that mankind had fallen from an original state of perfection and was still on the incline to Gehenna. The conception of an ascending growth, or in fact of any growth whatever, is a modern discovery. But with all our modern ideas we are not to assume that growth is always upward or forward. There were periods of decay in civilization, and it was just as proper for Gibbon to write of the decline and fall of the Roman Empire as for Motley to depict the rise of the Dutch Republic. It is the order of change that is to be sought, regardless of any definition of the word *progress*.

In the midst of the multitudinous data which accumulate in the course of an investigation, the genetic point of view helps to determine what shall be omitted. This is often a hard thing to do, for after a laborious aggregation of facts the investigator feels that every item is his own child and to leave any behind is nothing less than infanticide. The pages of history have been much encumbered with this paternal solicitude. Matters which have no intimate connection with the development of the period or the theme have no place in an historical narrative.

Coming to strictly practical considerations, we find this to be the situation of the hour. A large number of men and women are engaged in research in small sections of history in one or another of the social sciences. To obtain the best results in each case, it is incumbent upon every investigator to think carefully over the definition of history. The history of nations, or of any branch of thought, must be regarded as a part of the general history of civilization, and the contents of it written in that perspective. Likewise the smaller theme should not be a solitary fragment, but a contribution to the larger subject of which it is a part. Viewing his theme in this light the investigator finds a guide to the kinds of material needed, the choice of those to be used or discarded, and the form of their final presentation.

II

TESTING THE MATERIALS

It is not necessary in the twentieth century to repeat that no conclusions are of any value either in
natural science or in history unless these are based
on actual facts or reliable reports. But, while we
have passed beyond the age of naïve credulity, there
still remains the risk of accepting historical data without complete evidence of genuineness, or without
sufficient test of the competency of the witnesses.
Furthermore, the art of forgery has not disappeared,
and while forged productions nowadays enjoy only a
short life, the historian should be prepared to decide,
for example, whether new-found letters of Abraham
Lincoln are genuine or literary inventions. Many
questions about medieval and modern documents
have not yet been satisfactorily answered.

Historical research depends upon narratives, documents, remains, all left behind by some one other
than the investigator, and the procedure is the testing of the evidence of human beings and things. One
trouble for the beginner, and perhaps others, is that
he may not think of all the means and methods by

which this testimony may be evaluated; hence the importance of preparatory studies which give, at least in outline, the instruments and guides which are used in this kind of work. It may be that some of them will not come into immediate use in the field in which the student is at work, but the hints coming from different processes and other areas of history may lead to discoveries not thought of at first. Appreciation of evidence grows with practice, and a survey of the whole field should place in proper perspective the various arts and sciences which have come to the aid of historical research, with an increased respect for the experts whose labors are at our command.

If one should assemble in one place all the errors, prevarications, deceits, and major forgeries committed in the name of history, the work would fill a formidable series of volumes and become a severe indictment of human records and the human race itself. So much of this has occurred that men have said from time to time that the whole thing was a compound of deceit, a tissue of "lies agreed upon." When Napoleon thus expresses himself after his own masterly efforts in prevarication we can understand his pessimism, but a like opinion by the historian Fustel de Coulanges might give us pause if it were not clear that he did not follow that precept in his own writings. The student of the middle ages is apt to entertain a gloomy view of his predecessors, but there is another side which must not be forgotten.

18

The mistakes of historical writers are vastly more numerous than their deliberate attempts to deceive. Their limited knowledge, their credulity and lack of critical inquiry, have been the causes of error and the perpetuation of it. At the same time a great quantity of indisputable fact has come down from the past through the narratives of writers supported by documentary and archæological evidence. The transmission of this body of knowledge by manuscript, by copies, or by printing stands proved, so that the task which remains is to sift out the errors and misconceptions and to estimate the value of the contents.

Editors and commentators give much space in their writings to the variations of texts, as they should do in the attempt to reach the original form, but a large part of this discussion is of indifferent weight, or of more value to philology than to history. Long ago Isaac Taylor, writing of the transmission of ancient literature through the middle ages, said:

The actual amount and the importance of these corruptions of the text of ancient authors is likely to be overrated by general readers. . . . By far the greater number of all "various readings"—perhaps nineteen out of twenty—are purely of a verbal kind, and they are such as can claim the attention of none but philologists and grammarians; a few may deserve the notice of every reader of ancient literature; and a few demand the consideration of the student of history. But, taken in the mass, the light in which they should be regarded is that of their furnishing a significant and conclusive

19

proof of the care, fidelity, and exactness with which the business of copying was ordinarily conducted.[1]

The procedure by which it is determined whether a given source is genuine and admissible as evidence has been classified as External Criticism. This is fundamental, for if the document is fraudulent, or erroneously named or placed, no conclusions can be properly drawn from it. To make it competent testimony its origin and transmission must be clarified; if it is anonymous, an author is to be sought, or his sources of information uncovered. Whether narrative, document, or relic, the time and place must be determined to show how near it is to the situation described. The legality of a document, whether official or private, needs inquiry, and any other outside appearances demand the aid of palæography, chronology, and the other auxiliary sciences. Determination of these points, however, is not confined to externals, for the contents may reveal by the language, the local statements or preferences, the direct references, or even by the omissions and mistakes the answers to some of these preliminary questions.

The genuineness of a document having been established, there follows the process of weighing the testimony. Are the statements trustworthy or doubtful, probable or possible, or must they be thrown out? There are degrees of probability, and truth may

[1] Taylor, *Transmission of Ancient Books to Modern Times*, p. 20.

appear in one statement and not in another by the same man. Error is a constant companion of writers, and the determination of the amount of truth in historical materials has been labeled Internal Criticism, of which more will be said later.

However necessary these two divisions of preliminary operations, it cannot be reiterated too emphatically that criticism is not the end and object of historical research. So much labor and time has been devoted to the minutiæ of externals and argumentative conflict has so frequently ensued that it has often been forgotten that the real aim should be the interpretation of the contents of the document and their application to the immediate theme, as well as to the larger areas of history.

When examining a collection of historical materials it is easy to decide to which class the prominent specimens belong. A chronicle or a biography is an attempt to perpetuate a record of events, while a battle-ax or a silver coin is a voiceless relic of a period or a person named in the written accounts or found without any specific connection. The difference is clear, for the chronicle is a conscious effort to transmit information, while the battle-ax is unconscious testimony to the art of warfare. Upon this basis one is able to estimate the respective values of the two and interpret their contributions to the truth. Annals and relics are both the handiwork of man, but the one is subject to the errors, misconceptions, and mental peculiarities of the writer, while the other is an implement which he made for a special purpose without thought of the future. In both cases, however, we are obliged to make sure that the article is genuine and for that purpose to call in the aid of the sciences auxiliary to research.

The most primitive forms of consciously transmitted history are to be found in the materials which have come down through oral tradition. Ballads, tales, anecdotes, and sagas had a long existence both before and after the use of writing, and all of them show that it was the intention of the minstrels and story-tellers to give true accounts of the adventures of their heroes or their races. How much of this was the embellishment of poetical license is another matter, but there is no question about the intention, and these productions must be examined in order to see if historical fact is somehow embedded in them. The early traditions of European peoples have been industriously gathered up, and those of existing primitive tribes are being steadily collected, so that to-day this material can be found in print. At one time historians laid down the principle that impossible or miraculous statements should be discarded, while the possible or probable might be accepted as history. This method affords no security, and other investigators, like Niebuhr in Roman history, would throw out the whole body of early tradition. Neither plan will satisfy the requirements of scientific research, for traditions are in the first place monuments of early culture which contribute to the study of civilization and furthermore they often display in their language or their descriptions a geographical position, a racial movement, or some other point which fits in with known history. The discoveries of archæology, the science of language, and the principles of anthropology can in many cases be used to test the value of tradition and give it its true place among historical materials.

Chronicles, biographies, memoirs, diaries, genealogies—these leave no doubt as to their conscious intention to transmit information. Certain other human productions attempt the same rôle without saying a word. Historical paintings, portraits, scenic or portrait sculpture, designs and figures on ancient coins belong in this class. This pictorial art has suffered much from the unrestrained imagination of the artists. The early English depicted the court of King David in Anglo-Saxon costume, and Paul Veronese set the marriage at Cana in a magnificent Italian palace with his own contemporaries as guests, the intention in both cases being doubtless sincere. Later artists have not sinned so much in resurrecting the past. Tissot spent years in Palestine studying Hebrew and Arabic types, with the result that his illustrated Bible seems like contemporary history. We are greatly indebted to him for this vivid revival of ancient scenes, but we have to accept him as a scientific historian rather than as a witness. On the other hand, when the artist David ceased painting ancient Romans long enough to portray the coronation of Napoleon, the product enters another category and his work is to be tested as one would examine a witness in court. So it is with other forms of historical art, the first act being to prove that it is a genuine work of the artist, or of the period to which it is ascribed, and the second to decide how near he stood to the event, or how well he could be informed about it.

A list of relics giving unconscious testimony of the past would fill the catalogue of an archæological museum, but it also includes a number of things which are products of the mind as well as the hand. Not only human skeletons, pottery, arrow-heads, implements, and fine arts but also language, institutions, literature, and laws are in one aspect relics, alongside of deeds, contracts, and business records. All of these figure among historical materials from earliest Egypt to the present day, and it is the duty of the investigator to test the genuineness of each and see to it that each is duly assigned to its proper class. It is not always at first obvious that a newspaper contains both conscious accounts of political meetings and unconscious relics in the form of advertisements, nor that the preamble of a statute is the intentional excuse, good or bad, for the passage of the act, while the law itself is a monument of its period.

Certain other materials which are primarily relics

may have qualities that make them conscious history. A Celtic cromlech is a simple relic of an ancient burial custom; a gravestone with the name of William Brown is likewise only a monument, but when his birth and death have been added history begins; and when his services and admirable qualities have been spread over the marble, the gravestone has been converted into a document which calls for a different critical estimate. Not only epitaphs but many kinds of inscriptions, monuments, and certain forms of public documents contain these double characteristics. A Babylonian brick recording the building of a temple at Erech, a leaden tablet buried by French explorers on the banks of the Ohio, an epitaph from a New England graveyard, the obituary column of a newspaper—all of these need to be tested as historical statements consciously transmitted.

An interesting discussion might be opened over the value of tombstone poetry. The peculiar characteristics, the national differences, the persistence of certain forms, the presence of humor in the midst of universal vacuity lead one to qualify these products as literary relics. In spite of the oft-repeated "When this you see remember me," it is more charitable to ascribe such verses to survivors rather than to the defenseless departed, while the choice of selections may have been controlled by the width of the tombstone or the contents of the newspaper scrap-book. Trivial as it may seem at first glance, the matter is an item in the estimate of racial characteristics at a most solemn moment.

In conclusion it is hardly necessary to repeat that the most fundamental part of historical investigation is the test of genuineness of the materials obtained, and that the next important step is the classification which decides whether these offer conscious or unconscious testimony. When this preliminary work has been done, when we have decided that the document or the relic is genuine, the ground has been cleared for further serious labor. Proving that a chronicle or report is genuine gives no proof of the value of the testimony in its contents, nor does the fact that it is conscious testimony. The value must be estimated according to the personality of the author, the circumstances under which it was written, and other factors of internal evidence. As an introduction to methods of external criticism there follow brief outlines of the auxiliary sciences called upon to sift and clarify these materials.

III

DIPLOMATICS

The ancient word *diploma,* meaning originally a pair of folded wax tablets, has given the name to that branch of knowledge which deals with the forms of documents. *Document* in common usage is applied to almost anything containing historical data, like the word *Urkunde* in German speech, but in the science of diplomatics the term should not include chronicles or letters or epitaphs, but should be confined to written evidences of some legal transaction. Deeds, contracts, charters, privileges, court decisions, and similar actions are therefore the subjects of this study, and to forms and contents of these an immense amount of research has been devoted.

At first thought one might suppose that these matters might be left entirely to the experts in this field. As a matter of fact we must draw heavily upon their findings, but it will soon become evident that even the ordinary investigator needs to know something about the official formalities of his period and to be able to analyze a document, so that he may decide which parts are more historically valuable, which are expressions of will or relations of fact, and which are merely notarial repetitions. The reader who depends on printed copies only must equally be informed as to practices of chanceries and the construction of documents.

As the field is very large, and as the student usually confines his labors to one small period at a time, this chapter will be limited to a general outline of the science of diplomatics. Illustrative examples may be cited from early periods, but practice in the analysis of such documents will reveal in modern materials the difference between their essential and nonessential portions.

The official source of a paper is of the highest importance because we learn from that the legal weight of the instrument and because, knowing the particular practices of that office, we are furnished with an array of data by which to decide whether the document is genuine or a forgery. Intensive study of every period of European history and government has accumulated a store of data respecting chanceries and public officials; hence, in the case of France or the Holy Roman Empire, the organization period by period can be seen, the nature of the documents, the weight of the various signatures, and the historical significance can be estimated. Changes in the titles and qualities of persons, laymen or ecclesiastics, variations in the names of persons and places as time progresses—all these have produced a vast amount of information extremely valuable for the criticism of documents, but the investigator is not obliged to know it all at once when studying a limited period. Emphasis is laid upon this phase of research by all writers on diplomatics and for English history is clearly set forth by Mr. Hubert Hall in his *Studies in English Official Historical Documents*.

As an example of the difference between documents we may take a gift or transfer which reads "I, Henry, king, . . . grant to William abbot of B—— the lands and tenements hereinafter described." This is the *carta* in the technical sense and when properly signed and attested is a legal act giving full title to property. On the other hand, there may be found a document which reads something like a letter beginning with the words "Know all men by these presents that *we have granted* to the monastery of B—— . . ." This is the writ or *notitia*, and it furnishes as good title to the property as the other although it is not the act itself but rather a confirmation of it.

These distinctions throw light on the processes of law and are also important in the study of general historical questions because the time and place of the document may depend on its nature. The writ or confirmation may not follow immediately upon the issue of the *carta*, and inferences from the transaction may depend upon the nearness or remoteness of the announcement. The method of preparation, the signatures required, and other formalities may differ in the two documents and thus provide a variety of data for the proof of genuineness as well as the character of such acts.

Private acts as distinct from those of governments have been classified so that one may ascertain the forms used from time to time. It is evident that books of model forms were constantly in use and that for this reason the construction of a deed of sale or gift or mortgage changed very slowly except in minute details. These forms need to be consulted for the period under investigation.

In spite of the manifold usages and forms in which legal documents appear, there are characteristic subdivisions in them which are capable of classification. These parts or phrases may not all appear in the same act, but some of them will inevitably be present. Some are purely formal, while others contain the historical matter sought; consequently the distinctions must be kept in mind if the instrument is to be correctly interpreted.

In legal documents there are two general divisions of the contents. One introduces with formal phrases of politeness the persons who are parties in the transaction and give the details of the time, place, and witnesses to the act. The other division contains the text or statement of what is actually transacted. The first is called the protocol, and as part of the details are at the beginning and part, as the date, are at the end, they are sometimes classified as the initial protocol and the final protocol respectively. The initial protocol includes:

1. The Invocation, an appeal to Deity either by a symbol or in words, or by both methods at the same time. At first the symbol was a plain cross, or the combined initials PX, whence was derived the name *chrismon* for that emblem. This monogram in the eighth and ninth centuries became a curious snarl of lines in which the letter C may or may not have been visible, but was, nevertheless, an act of reverence. In the making of these signs there was so much individual ingenuity displayed that the chrismon is very useful in identifying the hands of different scribes and offices.

Variety appears also in the form of the verbal invocation, but the usage in a given chancery was so continuous and the changes were so slow that the phrases employed can assist but little in distinguishing one period from another. If it was the practice in one place to begin *In nomine domini et sanctæ trinitatis* the office would so continue rather than use *In nomine domini Jesu Christi dei æterni,* or *In nomine sanctæ et individuæ trinitatis*.

2. The Title is the part which gives the name and style of the grantor. "Charles by grace of God king of the Franks and Lombards" was the title of Charlemagne at one point, while later he added "Patrician of the Romans," and after 800 *imperator augustus*. So with other sovereigns all through the middle ages

there were changes which have been classified and dated. By means of these details the investigator may determine the period of an undated document and detect forgeries when the proper usage has been overlooked. The claims made in these phrases are not always historically correct, for the kings of England for a long time called themselves kings of France when they had no power in that country, but the official habit had its definite beginning and end, a fact which provides material for the criticism of documents and for historical inferences.

3. The Address or Inscription gives the names of the person or persons for whom the document is intended.

4. The Greeting or Salutation is often the single word *salutem* or "Greeting in the Lord" or, from a pope, "Greeting and apostolic benediction."

These four parts when present form the opening phrases of a legal instrument and are followed by the text or real substance of the act. Here also are important subdivisions which for purposes of criticism must be studied separately. Not all of them appear at the same time in every document. One or more may be absent or may be so blended as to make one sentence, yet somewhere the features which follow will be found and their nature should be understood.

1. The Preamble, Arenga, or Proem is usually a pious phrase, maxim, or expression of an obvious

truth inserted as a motive for the issue of the document. Neither the presence nor the absence of this would have any effect on the legality of the act, but the words add something of solemnity to the procedure.

"It is the duty of imperial highness not only to preserve inviolate the pious acts of his ancestors, but also to confirm them in all haste by his own authority." (Otto I, 966.) "Whatever things are done in time disappear with time unless they receive either testimony or memory confirmed by writing." "Since the flight of time causes forgetfulness in men . . ." "Since death and ignorance prevail among mortals the deeds of men ought to be committed to letters lest the weakness of failing memory should cause unforeseen contests." Variations on the importance of written testimony, or quotations from Scripture, serve as introductions.

2. The Publication or Promulgation is the sentence in which the act is announced. "Let it be known to all and every . . ." "Let it be known to all our faithful, present as well as future . . ." The phraseology differs widely and, in fact, may be omitted entirely.

3. The Narration explains why this particular document was issued and varies much in length and detail. It is the real preamble to the act and may be taken as the public motive. As such it is subject to inquiry as to whether it gives the actual motive or merely an

excuse. One should not assume an attitude of general hostility to such opening remarks, but at this point they enter the realm of historical narrative and become subject to verification or correction.

If the grantees have laid before the issuing authority earlier documents showing their rights, the act takes the form of a confirmation. It is often stated that "we have seen" these evidences and in such a case the act is classified as an *inspeximus*. In a confirmation of this kind the narration may contain valuable historical matter concerning the relations of the parties and may mention, or even give the contents of, documents which are otherwise unknown.

Another element appears in the narration when the name or names of those who requested the grant are given. This is sometimes classified as the Petition, and the persons as the *intervenientes*. The petition may have come from the grantee alone, or from some personage of influence, as when Otto III says "on account of the love and intervention of our beloved grandmother Adelheid" or "through the intervention of our councilor Bishop Cumanus." Or a group may be included, as "by the intervention of our most beloved wife Bertha, consort of our kingdom and our bed, and of our chief men, Liemar, Bishop of Bremen . . ." (Henry IV, 1077).

Sometimes this takes a more general form: ". . . we by divine inspiration and the intervention of our faithful subjects." In the course of time the words *consilio, consultu, consensu,* and similar terms came into use, and if we should follow the matter up we should find the *intervenientes* eventually present as witnesses necessary to the validity of the document. It is sufficient to say here that the petition appears in German imperial documents in the tenth century and that its development covers a long period.

4. The Disposition is the declaration of the will of the grantor. In this will be found the meat in the cocoanut. As a means of identification of the document it presents difficulties because the writer was not bound by formularies such as governed other parts of the procedure. There was a wish to be expressed, and there was complete freedom of language in making declarations of many different kinds; but in the disposition one finds the object of the document, and this is one of the reasons why a knowledge of the subdivisions of such a paper is most convenient to possess. When one is satisfied from other data that a series of documents is genuine, it saves much time in examination to put the eye at once upon that portion which contains the historical facts without reading all of the preparatory matter or the formal closing phrases. Facility in skipping is not difficult to acquire.

Yet one must not expect to find the subdivisions of the text always clearly marked. The grammatical construction may combine the narration with the disposition. The publication formula, or even the narration, may be absent. When older documents are presented for confirmation, the matter enacted may be entirely in the narrative recital of the contents of those documents, while the disposition is reduced to a phrase like: "In view of these facts we hereby decree. . . ." Nevertheless the analysis of the instrument points out the essentials to be sought.

5. The Sanction or *comminatio* is the penal clause in which punishment is threatened for the non-observance of the act. Such a threat is most likely to appear in a document issued by a sovereign or some other authority having the power to execute it, yet private grantors might indulge in maledictions against transgressors equivalent to signs reading "beware." The king might simply declare his displeasure or fix a fine for disobedience. Severe punishments were more likely to be specified in ecclesiastical documents, for the clergy had at command the penalties of both temporal and spiritual worlds and were provided with an abundant vocabulary in Deuteronomy and the 108th Psalm. Blessings for the obedient and Gehenna for malefactors were liberally distributed. Henry II of Germany in 1012 declared, "If any one indeed shall be tempted to infringe upon this our decree of immunity, which we do not believe will occur, let him prepare to pay one hundred pounds of pure gold." In 1063 a German bishop fortified a mortgage with this threat:

36

If any one shall infringe upon these matters by evil machination of fraud in any form whatever, if he does not respect a third warning, him we denounce by the authority of Almighty God and our anathema, and deprive him of his heritage in the kingdom of God.

These severe imprecations are characteristic of the earlier medieval period. In the twelfth century the papacy attempted to soften the practice by forbidding the clergy to use such threats in their contracts. The change was slow, but from the thirteenth century on such drastic spiritual penalties appear only in very weighty ecclesiastical documents and papal acts, where they are limited to threats of divine anger, deposition, and excommunication.[1]

6. The Corroboration is the clause which gives notice that the document is authenticated by signatures or seals which follow. The forms used were various, but whether short or long they came to the same effect. "Moreover that this free gift may remain unbroken and unimpaired, we have ordered it to be corroborated with the protection of the present seal." "And that it may remain fixed throughout posterity and among men who are lovers of truth I annex the seal of my royal authority and mark with my own hand the sign of the cross of the Lord."

The final protocol includes the factors which give authentication and force to the instrument. Without

[1] Giry, *Manuel de diplomatique.*

37

the formalities at the beginning which name the persons and those at the end of the document which give time, signature, and other forms of confirmation, the act would have had no legal value in its day, and for the historian would be only a curious scrap of parchment. Dates and chronology as well as seals will be treated in separate chapters, so space will be taken at this point for a few comments on signatures.

Important public documents are likely to have the signature of the sovereign or other grantor, but there are also multitudes of acts which depend upon signatures of subordinate officials or upon seals alone, even when they are royal grants. This condition is also evident in medieval private deeds and contracts where the seal may be the only authentication. Hence there is a great variety of situations to be encountered and it is important to know contemporary official duties and responsibilities as well as the phraseology introducing the signature. Upon these subjects the experts have assembled a vast amount of special data for which only indications can be given here.

In official documents it is necessary to take note of

(1) the signature of the grantor, king, bishop, etc.;

(2) signatures of chancery officials; and

(3) signatures of persons who witness or consent to the act.

The proof of a signature is naturally palæographic, and upon this topic an abundance of evidence in the way of monographs and facsimiles is available. Even when kings could not write, the marks they made in monograms formed by others have been identified and established.

The use of the monogram, for example, had an interesting history. The Merovingian kings could write and made use of the monogram only in exceptional cases. The Carolingians, however, had not acquired that art; hence their secretaries drew curious combinations of the letters of their baptismal names, and royalty completed the puzzle with a short pen-stroke or a blot. This practice continued for a long time after kings and emperors were fully able to write. For example, the monogram of the German Henry III in 1040 occupied some five square inches of space, and high ecclesiastics used similar devices. In the course of time the real autograph appeared, and still later the monogram returned as an additional ornament.

When the royal signature was only a mark, it was necessary to add the signature of a chancery official to give the document legal authentication. This office grew in importance till it became indispensable even when sovereigns could write, and there enters a constitutional situation of much interest in the development of law-making, as well as a quantity of palæographical data to be used in the identification of manuscripts.

Other witnesses to public and private papers are

interesting both from the point of view of proof and as sources of historical information. At an earlier period these persons were regarded as intercessors or advisers and one might think they served to justify the act, but gradually they are transformed into witnesses as we understand the term and are so designated in public and private papers. As to actual signatures there was wide variety in practice; in many instances the names alone are given as if the persons named were ocular witnesses of the transaction and might be called upon to testify if necessary. This idea is confirmed in the frequent use of the words "and many others," added to the list. Among more than a thousand deeds formerly belonging to Battle Abbey examined by the writer only one medieval contract contained signatures of witnesses; in the others they were simply named.

From the names found in public acts we may infer who were influential persons about the court. As witnesses to a document of Edward written in 1061 there appear five bishops, two abbots, four dukes, four councilors, and ten minor officials. Sound Anglo-Saxon names they bore, each followed by the mark of a cross, which they may or may not have placed there themselves. So in many less elaborate instances persons may appear who are otherwise known, characters previously unknown may be discovered, and data as to time and place of the movements of courtiers may be incidentally revealed.

The foregoing analysis was applied to medieval materials, but it is equally important that the student of modern history be aware of the construction of his documents. Let him dissect a proclamation, a public grant, a private deed, a colonial charter, and other similar papers and separate the pure formalities from the essential facts. The medieval formalities may not all be present, but in spite of simplifications the modern document is based upon the same construction. Practice will give an understanding of legal validity, of tests of genuineness, as well as an insight into the historical setting. Mistakes in the valuation of this kind of evidence can be avoided by careful scrutiny of its parts.

IV

PALÆOGRAPHY

The study of handwriting lies at the foundation of all historical studies of periods previous to the invention of printing in the fifteenth century. A broad definition of "ancient writing" might include records of Egypt and Babylonia or of the Mayas of Central America, but as a matter of fact the term *palæography* is in practice chiefly confined to the study of manuscripts in Greek and Latin. Since the literatures of Greece and Rome have come down to us almost exclusively in manuscripts of the Christian era, it becomes a science of medieval chirography, with its various transformations and national developments. This does not overlook the fact that our alphabetical signs were derived from the more ancient hieroglyphs nor that the Greeks owed much to their predecessors, but the study of Epyptian and cuneiform writing as well as epigraphy in general is of such a special character that each is attached to its particular branch of archæology.

Furthermore, since Latin became the universal language for formal communication in western Europe, the study of its written forms is the most conspicuous part of palæography, and space will be taken here to indicate the nature of the science. It is not necessary that every investigator should become an expert palæographer, but it frequently happens that an important interpretation depends upon a doubtful phrase, and the student should at least be in a position to understand the argument of the expert when he transforms into print the riddles of medieval writing. Moreover, there are still many unexplored regions in documentary archives, and the investigator is frequently required to consult the unprinted matter of his period. In such a case one ought not to be terrified at the rather forbidding aspects of the matter, nor even at the word *palæography*, for it is not difficult to learn to read the handwriting of a given period, although judgment as to the authenticity of a document may require extended experience.

The letters which we use to-day are a heritage from the Romans, and they passed through a series of changes which continued until their forms were stabilized by the invention of movable type. Two lines of development were followed, one concerned with the preparation of formal books, and the other applied to the everyday requirements of the citizen, memoranda, business records, and eventually government documents. The book-hand starts with the Roman capital letters, such as are found on the monuments and most of which are much like modern type. For some centuries books of a literary, legal, or more or less permanent character were carefully spelled out in capitals one letter at a time. Even after changes had developed, the capitals were used for works of ancient and revered authors such as the Scriptures or Virgil's poems, evidently as a token of greater dignity. In the course of time this *capitalis elegans* underwent modifications which made the lines less rigid, and so from the fourth to the seventh century there appears also the *capitalis rustica* in books and public acts.

At the same time another kind of modification was going on whereby greater speed in writing was sought. The capitals continued as a rule to be of the same height, but their sharp corners were being rounded off, and other short cuts came into use. The letter *M,* for example, was formed as in our present script, and *H* lost its right arm and became *h.* This Uncial script, which is said to have come into use in the period of Diocletian, was followed by further modifications of the letters, which now ceased to be uniform in height, some of them extending above the level and some below on a scale of four parallel lines instead of two, as in the case of *b* and *p.* The capital letters in this script, however, prevail to such an extent that it is classified as Half-Uncial.

When the process had gone still further and all of the letters of the alphabet had either been modified in the interest of rapidity or adjusted to the scale

44

of four lines, the result was the Minuscule, which is equivalent to lower-case type. This point was reached in the Carolingian period, but centuries elapsed before adoption of the precise forms of letters with which we are familiar.

Evolution of the small letters was assisted by the presence of a cursive hand which was in use from the days of the Romans onward. Marks on the walls of Pompeii, notes on wax tablets, and other relics give evidence of a rapid hand which was used for memoranda or communications of a temporary character. This cursive also had its history running through modified capitals into minuscule, but it was a story of decadence toward illegibility until Charlemagne ordered a reformation and founded schools where writing was taught. Upon this basis were founded various national hands, the Carolingian, the Lombardic, the West Gothic, and others which helped to standardize the forms of letters and brought them into use not only for ephemeral memoranda but also for private and public acts of a permanent character. Deeds of land, imperial decrees, and papal documents were transmitted in writing which was less formal than that used for books but which, along with more rapid execution, had its own rules and regulations.

By the time of the Revival of Learning there had developed for the writing of Latin a book-hand of capitals and small letters which had been refined by studies of the best ancient examples on the part of humanistic scholars. On this was based the casting of movable type and thus from the middle of the fifteenth century the letters of the printed page became standardized. The written document was not so easily controlled, but the standards of government chanceries were slow to change, and styles of penmanship varied according to the dignity of the offices from which they emanated. Thus in England both before and after printing there were distinct forms, known as Court Hand (for various governmental acts), Chancery Hand (for the legal records of that court), and Secretary Hand (for another class of documents) as well as the individual peculiarities coming from local scribes writing in Latin or English. In modern German script the student will discover forms of letters which had a long history in the writing of Latin but followed a course of development differing from that of English script.

The foregoing is but a meager outline of the evolution of modern handwriting. Each period has been studied with meticulous care by experts. The peculiarities of each national hand and the forms of letters used in a given chancery from time to time have been described, and even the habits of an individual scribe are occasionally identified. Thus a large body of knowledge has been accumulated and fortified by descriptions and facsimiles. To become possessed of this requires careful study of the facts already acquired, with constant reference to the originals or reproductions. The way has been prepared by numerous writers of manuals, to which this chapter must refer the reader while space is taken for a little further consideration of the place of palæography in historical research.

The form of writing used in a given period is determined by dated documents of which the genuineness is certain. When undated documents are under consideration, naturally the first step is comparison with authentic originals, but numerous factors must be taken into account before attempting an answer. It must be remembered, first, that an official hand may and usually does last a long time as a matter of habit or routine and that certain peculiarities may continue over an extended period because of the special dignity or solemnity of the class of documents in which they are used, while in private papers or common use changes in chirography are taking place. Likewise in the more formal manuscripts of books the writer may have had before him models of a quite different age. Consequently palæographical data cannot be employed to establish the month or year of a manuscript, but only at best the period to which it belongs.

In England it is evident that there existed not only scribes connected with government offices but also in a multitude of places professional writers whose skill and peculiarities varied widely. The

47

fashions in letters of a given period can be classified in a general way, but we have to reckon with carelessness and haste, particularly in private records, as well as the fact that the hand of a scribe may change as he grows older. The facsimiles in Jenkinson's *Court Hand* show for the one year 1225 a wide variety of script. Hence for identification of time or place palæography is more important for corroboration than for direct evidence. The contents, the legal forms, the witnesses, the seals (if present), the writing materials, the watermarks where paper is employed, and perhaps other data must be studied when an anonymous undated document is under consideration. For all documents, indeed, the British palæographers proclaim with one voice that the most important aid is a knowledge of administrative methods, as seen in the proceedings of ministries, councils, or courts as they have historically developed.

At the same time palæography provides the only means for finding out the contents of a document, whether it be genuine or suspicious. Some one must know how to read it and thus be able to ascertain what the author intended to say. For this purpose a knowledge of the development of individual letters is important, for the letter *a* at one time is open at the top and at another looks like *cc* and the letter *t,* as written for a long time, might be taken for *c.* The capitals, likewise, go through an evolution which should be understood when curious forms are encountered. The initial letter of a difficult place name if not comprehended may bring the reader to a complete stop or to an erroneous interpretation.[1] Hence a familiarity with the writing of more than one period is highly important for readiness and security.

The most serious difficulty in reading medieval Latin comes from the abundant use of abbreviations. Owing to the costliness of parchment and the desire to economize space, the scribes habitually shortened many words by using only part of the letters, particularly in words and syllables which frequently recurred and were commonly understood. This was sometimes carried to extremes; a page of familiar terms in an account book may be filled with words of three or four letters—a condition which, by the way, may be found at the present day as well. Yet there were two underlying systems for abbreviation which came down to the middle ages from ancient Roman usage and were applied with very considerable regularity, in spite of conflicting tendencies.

The older form was abbreviation by Suspension, in which the first part of a word is written instead of the whole, as *Test.* for *testimentum,* or the first letter of each part, as *Nt.* for *noster.* Since this method gave no indication of the ending of the word, the case in which it was used would be in

[1] Hubert Hall, *Studies in English Official Documents,* p. 357.

doubt. Hence this system was used only in well-known terms, especially in legal forms. Abbreviation by Contraction indicated the word by the use of the first letter or letters and the last letter and often a significant letter from the middle, as *dns* for *dominus*, *eps* for *episcopus*, *nr* for *noster*. By this method the case ending and the number, singular or plural, could be indicated by the appropriate final letter. This system was an inheritance from classical times which gradually made its way over western Europe and reached Ireland and England in the eighth century. Contraction of familiar words came into universal use and the matter looks chaotic to the beginner until it appears that certain practices were common to all writers of Latin and the peculiarities can be classified. Strokes or signs were used for some conjunctions just as we write *&* and *etc*. The letter *i* placed over the first letter in *cmen* meant that *r* was omitted and the word was really *crimen*. The letter *p* with a dash over the top meant *pre* or *præ;* with a straight line through the leg it was *per, par,* or *por;* with a bow on its lower limb it was *pro,* and these abbreviations were prefixed to longer words like *phibition* or used as middle syllables as *corpalis* for *corporalis*. Attention also must be given to the Arabic numerals when present, for only half of them had taken on the forms with which we are familiar.

These few examples state the problems of abbreviation only in part. The subject must be worked out with the help of textbooks and facsimiles. The use of shortened forms occurs in so many situations with the various letters of the alphabet that dictionaries of abbreviations have been compiled which render indispensable aid. The matter looks complicated, but it can be surmounted with patient attention.

To recapitulate, the study of palæography is still necessary to the investigator of medieval and early modern history, whether political, legal, or social. Great quantities of documents have been printed, but vast numbers remain unpublished or merely listed. There is also much documentary matter which has been printed without extending the abbreviations, for example, the *Valor ecclesiasticus* of Henry VIII and some of the records of the Exchequer. Without a knowledge of the customs of the scribes these printed pages are unintelligible. Many curious mistakes, even ridiculous blunders, have been made through hasty reading of abbreviations, and the historian is compelled to take every precaution against error.

The importance of handwriting does not end with the invention of printing. Official documents and records continue to be made with pen and ink, but with an increasing uniformity in the shapes of the letters. Differences in personal habits and skill become more and more the criteria by which manuscripts are judged, and controversy is more likely to rise over words, rather than over the question whether the document is an authentic letter of the person whose name is signed.

The detection of fraud and forgery in modern handwriting has become almost a science. The methods employed are well worth study, not only for present use, but for the suggestions for clues and lines of evidence which may be applied to older material. These modern investigations, which are applied for the most part in criminal cases or testamentary litigation, include the physical examination of paper and instruments of writing as well as the chemical analysis of inks. All of these elements have their history in which periods of usage can be identified. The comparison of the disputed script with known documents brings in the questions of pen pressure, fineness of writing, the structure of lines and the overlapping of additions, all of which require the use of the microscope. Magnification may be needed also to determine the habits of the writer as to the slope of his script, the spacing of words and individual letters, the usual formation of his letters, and the relation of these to the base line.

Within recent years whole series of instruments have been devised for the study and scientific measurement of handwriting, paper, and ink. By means of the comparison microscope and Lovibond's Tintometer glasses it is possible to compare accurately the colors of inks. Another special type of microscope is used for examining opaque surfaces such as pen-strokes and this instrument gives paper a totally different appearance from that seen in ordinary daylight. The age of paper, especially of the later periods, can sometimes be closely ascertained through microscopic and chemical analysis of the materials used in its manufacture.

Quite new in connection with this task is the employment of infra-red light used photographically. Its chief value is in reading through expunged passages, for some substances used in erasure are quite transparent to this light, though others are too resistant to give results. With ultra-violet light, used either directly or photographically, erasures and alterations are easily detected and the light is applied for the restoration of faded writing, the detection of forgery, or the examination of palimpsests where one writing has been erased to give place to another. When the ultra-violet fails to render writing visible the result can often be reached by photography with light filters of various kinds.

Mere visual comparison of writing no longer has any standing in court when controverted by the microscope and the chemical test. Detailed explanations of the methods are available in convenient textbooks, and to the student of historical material, even when not expecting to become an expert witness

53

on handwriting, the questions treated are decidedly suggestive and sometimes vitally important.[2]

To illustrate a modern problem in chirography I may quote an example which was recently neatly worked out at the Huntington Library by Miss Norma B. Cuthbert of the manuscript department. The solution depended largely on familiarity with the writing of the persons concerned, but it also involved considerable research to determine their movements and the time when the matter was written. The manuscript was a small sheet of paper with fold marks and fragments of a seal showing that it had been the envelope or cover sheet of a letter. On one side was the address "To the Right Honorable, the Earl of Loudon, North America." On the same side, but on what would have been the back of the letter when folded, were the words in another hand, "from Sr. Cha. Hardy. 17th March, 1757." On the reverse of the sheet in still another hand was a list of eight forts beginning with Fort Cumberland, with the numbers of men in each. Check-marks in red ink before the names of the forts showed that some one had given the paper an examination. The problem was to decide who wrote these various endorsements and how they could have come together on the same sheet at that time.

[2] The subject is briefly handled—but widely extended through bibliographies—in C. A. Mitchell, *Documents and Their Scientific Examination* (London, 1922) and A. S. Osborn, *Questioned Documents* (Rochester, N. Y., 1910).

Knowing by experience the writing of many Revolutionary characters, it was evident to the investigator that the list of military posts was in the familiar hand of George Washington, but the address to the Earl of Loudon was written by Governor Henry Ellis of Georgia, and enough of the seal remained to show that it likewise came from the Governor. The words "from Sr. Cha. Hardy" were endorsed by Major General James Abercromby, whose papers are much in evidence in the Huntington collection. Where were these people about St. Patrick's Day of 1757?

Governor Ellis at that time was in Georgia. Governor Loudon about the middle of March set out from New York for Philadelphia, leaving General Abercromby in New York as temporary commander-in-chief. In that capacity he opened all letters before they were forwarded to Loudon in Philadelphia. On March 17, 1757, a large package was sent on from New York, the list of which still exists among the Loudon manuscripts. Item 12 in this reads "Letter from Gov. Ellis of Georgia by Sir Charles Hardy," so Abercromby's endorsement is accounted for. Sir Charles Hardy was in New York, and it appears that Governor Ellis had written to him enclosing a letter to the Earl of Loudon which Hardy had very properly turned over to General Abercromby to be forwarded to Philadelphia.

Furthermore, on March 17 Colonel George Washington arrived in Philadelphia, where he had come to consult his commander-in-chief. His interview with Loudon occurred on March 22. It is evident that Loudon requested him to give a list of his forces and he did so impromptu on the most convenient slip of paper at hand. The small red dashes were the check-marks which Loudon habitually used, as abundantly shown in his other papers. The document, therefore, was catalogued according to its most important contents under "Washington, Col. George."

WATERMARKS

When paper came into use for documents and books there came with it a means of identification which has proved very useful. A device of wire twisted into the outline of a hand, a star, a bunch of grapes, a unicorn, or one of a hundred other figures, was fastened in the bottom of the screen on which the paper was drained. The pressure at that point made the sheet a little thinner, and on holding it up to the light a translucent print of the mark could be discerned. The process continues to this day in the manufacture of the better class of writing-papers.

Considerable attention has been given to the history of this matter, but the field is so large that information is by no means complete. The most

elaborate treatment comes from a Swiss paper man-
ufacturer who devoted years to the compilation of
four quarto volumes of text and 60,000 devices
which show European watermarks from about 1282
to 1600. There is much to be found here respecting
the designs used in English papers, but that field still
requires more thorough investigation.

In paper made by the old hand method the wire
marks of the screen itself are usually plainly visible,
and the relation of the watermark to the perpendic-
ular and horizontal lines, as well as the size of the
figure, plays a part in the identification. Exact
measurement, therefore, is necessary before making
comparisons with the cuts in a reference book, for
these contain a bewildering number of sizes of the
same animal, or water-jug, or human hand. In Briquet's work, referred to above, the figures of the
same kind are assembled together and printed on
the same scale as the originals. So far as possible
the author has given the dates between which the
specimen was used and the place and name of the
paper-maker.

If the identification is exact you have, not a date,
but a period within which the document could have
been written. These periods are of different extent,
for a watermark may have lived five, ten, or fifteen
years and does not in itself reveal the year of its use
in a manuscript or book. Yet it is a valuable point
to have these limits, for they provide evidence as

to the general period of a genuine work and assist in the detection of forgeries. The extent of this latter crime has been very great. It began before paper came into general use and continues to this day, although the historian may not be concerned with all its forms. The literary counterfeit, made either for gain or for amusement, may come his way, and the evidences of paper and watermark are at his disposal. Modern forgers have been aware of the risks in the use of paper. One group of Shaksperian counterfeits were written on fly-leaves cut from books of the Elizabethan period but were nevertheless detected, while a more recent attempt to imitate the handwriting of Abraham Lincoln was —unfortunately for the forger—written on paper containing a watermark with the plain date of 1898.

V

CHRONOLOGY

The modern system of dating documents and historical events has become so much a habit of thought that it requires an effort to realize that time was not always measured in so simple a manner. The present generation writes 1930 or 1776 without further adornment except the day of the month. On going back a few hundred years, we are inclined to add for security the letters A. D., and for a still earlier period the initials B. C. But the term *year of our Lord* was not introduced in the calendar until more than five hundred of those years had elapsed and was not employed regularly in dating documents until centuries later than that.

The calendar of Julius Cæsar ruled the western world even long after Christianity had been adopted as the state religion of empire and nations, and consequently dates were fixed by the regnal years of kings or other high officials, with the months and days that were used by the Romans. Calculations made in the sixth century by a Christian monk, Dionysius, fixed the birth of Christ as in the year 754 after the founding of Rome. Earlier Christians had with greater probability made this 750 A. U. C., but the estimate of Dionysius came gradually into use, first in Italy and then for private papers in France in the eighth century and in Germany during the ninth. A Saxon charter of 676 is dated *ab incarnatione* "according to the recapitulation of Dionysius." In 816 the Council of Chelsea decreed that bishops should date their acts from the birth of Christ. The papacy itself did not adopt the Christian era till near the close of the tenth century, and the spread of its usage came about by imitation rather than by decree, for popes and kings considered the years of their reigns to be sufficient indication of time. For centuries after the use of *anno domini* became common in certain classes of documents, the regnal years were employed in other forms of record.

Owing to the absence of a standard method and the diversity of practice in a multitude of localities, the study of dates in medieval documents is a complicated matter, not because of difficult astronomical calculations but because of the uncertainty in the use of simple data in various regions. Writers on chronology, however, have come to the rescue with tables and lists which show provincial usages, such as the variations in the beginning of the year and the dates of saints' days. These are especially important for the Continental divisions of Europe. For example, one must distinguish between St. Elizabeth, mother of John the Baptist, whose day is November 5, and St. Elizabeth, widow of the King of Hungary, November 19, the latter date being used in English calendars. In Potthast's *Bibliotheca historica medii ævi,* Supplemental Volume, there are about 8,400 names of saints, martyrs, bishops, popes, etc., with dates which occur in historical writings. Brinckmeier's *Historische Chronologie* gives more than 1,000, and Bond's *Handy Book for Verifying Dates* has about 450 names and holy days commonly observed in England.

The great object of medieval calendars and time calculations was to fix the date of Easter and the movable holy days depending upon it. The fixed saints' days called for religious observances and were listed in their proper places, and even the hours of the day were measured and named from the various church services. Calculated and prepared by the clergy, the calendar bore throughout an ecclesiastical aspect, and as the same profession monopolized most of the learning and wrote the documents of the time, it is not surprising that secular acts should commonly be dated by their proximity to a holy day. Of saints there were more than enough in common observance to provide points of reference for every week in the year.

The year given most frequently was that of the reign of the ruling sovereign without direct indication of the *annus domini.* Translated specimens read

"Tuesday the feast of St. Lucia, virgin, in the reign of King Henry IV the xiv"; "Wednesday next after the feast of St. Hilarius 14 Henry IV"; "Sunday next after the feast of St. Valentine, 4 Edward III." St. Lucia Day is December 13. The fourteenth and last year of Henry IV began September 29, 1412, and consequently this December is of that year. The feast of St. Hilarius is January 13, and 14 Henry IV has gone over into 1413. To find the day of the month of the Wednesday following we must first ascertain on what day of the week January 13 fell in 1413. Tables and calendars are available which show the day of the week on which each medieval year began. It appears that 1413 began on Sunday; consequently January 13 fell on Friday, and the following Wednesday was January 18. St. Valentine's Day, then as now, was February 14; in the fourth year of Edward III, 1330, it fell on Wednesday, and the Sunday previous was February 11.

One may work out rapidly from these printed tables the dates indicated in early documents, but care must be exercised in their use, and the student should understand the terms employed and the nature of the calculations from which he has been relieved. So constant was the use of holy days instead of the day of the month that one important item in the medieval calendar cannot be overlooked. This was the system started in the sixth century which assigned to each day of the week one of the first seven letters of the alphabet. January 1 was always A, and if this occurred on Saturday the following Sunday would be B, or if the year started on Wednesday the next Sunday would be E and all the rest of the Sundays of the year would be the same. This was called the Sunday Letter, *littera dominicalis,* and from it the first day of any month, or in fact any day of the year, could be determined. To the ecclesiastic this method was important in fixing the date of Easter, while to the modern student seeking to find the day of the week of January 13, 1413, in order to fix the date of the next Wednesday, it saves a vast amount of circumlocution. He finds that the Year Letter is A, making Sunday the first and eighth of January, and hence that the thirteenth fell on Friday and the Wednesday after was the eighteenth of January.

Even that much calculation may be avoided, for chronologists have prepared tables for each Dominical Letter, or, in other words, a series of calendars each beginning the year with a different day of the week. Leap-years by adding a day change the order of the letters after February 24. If such a year began on Sunday, it would start with letter A, then change on February 26 to letter G for the remaining Sundays of the year. Seven more tables show the calendar for all possible leap-years, and all of them are easy to use when one knows the meaning of *littera dominicalis.*

Other tables give the date of Easter for the entire Christian era, or so simplify the matter that no extended calculation is required. Even the dates of the holy days in Lent have been tabulated for all possible dates of Easter and have thus removed the difficulties in finding the day when related to one of these movable feasts.

The time questions thus far mentioned do not cover all of the data to be found in medieval documents, and a few more examples will show some of the problems which may be encountered. The following date from a movable feast uses two items of identification; "Tuesday after the first Sunday in Lent called *invocavit* . . . 1460." An Easter table shows that Easter fell on April 13 in 1460 (a leap-year), Ash Wednesday on February 27, and the first Sunday in Lent on March 2; consequently the following Tuesday was March 4. The given Sunday is further identified by the first word of the music with which the mass began on that day, *invocavit*. These services followed an invariable order, and hence the first words or *introitus* establish absolutely the Sundays of the year and are frequently used alone for that purpose, as "Monday after the Sunday *quasimodo geniti*," meaning the first Sunday after Easter. Occasionally the gospel of the day was used for the same purpose. A list of *introitus* with dates is usually given in books on chronology.

In formal documents still other data are fre-

quently included. The following from the records of
Geneva contains about as many items as will be
found in one place. Partly transliterated it reads, "In
the year after the incarnation of the Lord MCLV,
lord Adrian Pope, happily presiding over the Holy
Roman Church, in the reign of Frederick, Emperor,
*vi kalendas Martii, anno bisextile, feria vii, luna xxx,
indictione iii, cyclus lunaris et solaris xvi, epacta
xxvi, concurrentes vii.*" Several of these items are
merely confirmatory of others, and at first glance
there seem to be contradictions. Thus 1155 is not a
leap-year, *anno bisextile. Feria vii,* the seventh day
of the week, is Saturday, and we may safely assume
that the scribe would put that down correctly. The
vi kalendas of March in a leap-year is February 25,
and fits exactly on Saturday in 1156. This contradic-
tion is explained when we note the local usage for
the beginning of the year. In Geneva up to 1305 the
year began at Easter, which in 1156 occurred on
April 15; consequently the scribe considered himself
in 1155 when he wrote this document, and included
the words *indictione iii* which apply to that year.

The Indiction was a cycle of fifteen years, an old
Roman institution, confirmed in law by Constantine
in 312 A. D. for purposes of taxation. These cycles
were not named or numbered, but the number given
is that for the year in the existing cycle. Tables of
indictions are provided, but a simple calculation will
suffice. Subtract 312 from the given year and divide

65

by 15. In this case $1155 - 312 = 843 \div 15 = 56$ with the remainder 3, the indiction iii given by this scribe, whose year is 1155 until Easter.

The calculation may require further attention in certain cases, for there were three dates in use in the middle ages for the beginning of the cycle. The Greek or Constantinople indiction began September 1. The Imperial or Cæsarian from 312 A. D. began September 24, while the Roman or Pontifical indiction started from December 25, or from January 1, 313. There was great irregularity of usage, and consequently slight differences in dates in the latter part of the year may occur and local practice must be taken into account. On the whole the indiction is the most valuable factor for the corroboration of the given Christian year, as it is a steadfast item in the chaos of medieval time-keeping and survived long in important documents.

In old calendars the months were assigned alternately thirty and twenty-nine moons or lunations, so that *luna xxx* in this case stands for March and is a purely ornamental confirmation of the previous expression "kalends of March." This lunar cycle is a circuit of the moon through all its phases to the point where they occur again on the same days of the month. This happens once every nineteen years, and the calculation was an inheritance from antiquity introduced into the calendar in the sixth century A. D., harking back to an act of the Council of Nicæa

66

of 325. The count of cycles begins with a year when the new moon occurred on January 1. Such a year was 1 B. C. and this was taken as the starting point for medieval chronology; hence to find the position of any Christian year in this cycle it is simply necessary to add 1 and divide by 19. In this case 1155 + 1 = 1156 ÷ 19 = 60 with the remainder 16, the *cyclus lunaris* given above. This may not coincide with the astronomical new moon by as much as two days, but the difference was compensated in the course of a long period. The cycle number was called the Golden Number, perhaps because written in the calendars in bright letters, and is much used as a key to other data.

The solar cycle is a period of twenty-eight years in which the days of the month go through all possible relations to the days of the week, returning at the end of the cycle to the same relation as at the beginning, with, for instance, January 1 again falling on Sunday. The starting point taken by the medieval calculators was the year 9 B. C. when the cycle began on Monday; consequently to find the cycle number it is necessary to add 9 to the date before dividing by 28. In this case 1155 + 9 = 1164 ÷ 28 = 41 with remainder 16, giving the *cyclus solaris xvi.*

Concurrentes were factors used chiefly in calculations for Easter Sunday but were employed also, as in this case, for the corroboration of other dates.

As common years have fifty-two weeks and one day, and leap-years fifty-two weeks and two days, the name *concurrentes* was applied to one or both of these surplus days because they "concur" or run alongside the solar cycle. Concurrents give inevitably the day of the week on which March 24 occurs and consequently, by further calculation, the first day of any month. For such purposes the days of the week are given numbers from one to seven beginning with Sunday; hence *concurrentes vii* in this example stands for Saturday, as already stated by *feria vii*.

Epact is a word of Greek origin meaning "something added," and in medieval chronological usage was applied to the excess of the solar year over the lunar, a matter of eleven days. In dating it means practically the age of the moon on January 1 of the given year and determines the date of the full moon from which Easter Sunday was calculated. Tables of epacts were in use from early times and are given in modern works, so that calculation may be avoided. Both tables and computation show the year to be 1156 in this example, as it would be in Geneva at Easter.

After consideration of all these data the editors of this document have justified themselves in giving it the date of February 25, 1156.[1]

We observe in this problem that the beginning of the year is an important factor in the fixing of a

[1] *Sources du Droit Suisse* (Genève), I, No. 8.

date. Not only Easter but three other days were used as the starting point. The ancient Roman year began on January 1, and its twelve divisions have continued with little change. The calendar of Dionysius originating in the sixth century also started from January 1, but theological questions entered into the matter. Chroniclers interpreted the word *incarnation* as indicating the day of the conception, and consequently March 25 became for them the beginning of the year. Others insisted that the actual birth of Christ was the real *incarnatio dei* and so dated the year from December 25. The religious importance of Easter is quite understandable, but as it was a movable feast its use as the first day of the year made it one of the plague-spots of medieval chronology. Local usage must be consulted in all these cases. Even the Gregorian Calendar, with the adoption of January 1 and all its astronomical corrections, did not at once abolish confusion as to the beginning of the year, as the nations were slow in adopting the new plan. The point of change in each country must be carefully noted.

In England from the seventh to the thirteenth century the popular year began with Christmas, but somewhere in the twelfth century the church began also to reckon from March 25, and by the fourteenth both clergy and laity had gradually come to use the latter date. The old Roman reckoning from January 1 was not forgotten, but was spoken of as the "historical year," while the legal year for both church and state was calculated from March 25, the feast of the Annunciation. Even after the reformation of the calendar in 1582 the British held on in this confusion for six generations and changed to the present system in 1752. This accounts for the double dates frequently used in books written since that time when the event occurred between January 1 and March 25. For instance, Archbishop Laud was executed January 10, 1645, but the official year was still 1644; hence for security it may be written January 10, 1644/45.

The hours of the day are not usually important in a document even when included in a date, but they constantly recur in chronicles and narratives, and the meaning of the nomenclature must be kept in mind. The division of the day into two periods of twelve hours each was inherited from Roman antiquity, but the parts commonly used were named after the canonical hours prescribed for church services. The hour of sixty minutes lay dormant until public clocks became common in the fourteenth and fifteenth centuries and the modern expressions of time came into regular use. The canonical hours in their relation to the astronomical day were subject to change in practice, and hence calculations to the minute are out of the question, but the fundamental divisions were as follows:

70

Matutina, originally from midnight to 6 A. M.
Prima, 6 A. M. to 9 A. M.
Tertia, 9 A. M. to 12 M.
Sexta, 12 M. to 2 or 3 P. M.
Nona, 2 or 3 P. M. to 4 P. M.
Vespera, 4 P. M. to 7 P. M.
Completorium was the final service of the day, at about 7 P. M.

Certain of the services in the course of time came to be sung together, with the general result of pushing all of them back to an earlier hour, and the result was that in everyday usage the chief periods of the day came to be *prima, tertia, nona,* and *vespera. Nona* was the time for the midday meal, but with all the variations in practice we are not entitled to imagine that all of Europe sat down to dinner at the same hour. Approximation is the best that can be obtained when expressions of time are given in canonical hours.

Space cannot be given to the many questions which arise when a date is omitted and the time must be derived from internal evidence. Sometimes the witnesses can be traced, especially if they held office. Sometimes earthquakes serve as era-marks, like the one at Basel in 1356 which provided both a "before-and-after" event and a moral warning for many years. Movements of the earth cannot be predicted or calculated backward, but the eclipses which are often mentioned in the chronicles have been tabulated by the astronomers for the whole Christian era and are available for the control of historical statements. Many of these problems occur in the investigation of forged documents and have been discussed elsewhere.

Our present calendar is due to a reformation undertaken and promulgated by an enlightened pope, and called "Gregorian" after him. The discrepancy between the old calendar and the solar reckoning had long been observed, and the difference had gradually amounted to ten days. After calculations by an expert commission, the accumulation of surplus minutes, due to the fact that the old calendar inherited from the Romans gave the year 365 days and 6 hours, was adjusted by deducting ten days. A papal decree directed that the day following October 4, 1582, should be called October 15, and various minor changes included a different reckoning of leap-year. This omission of ten days, provided in round numbers for popular convenience, was not mathematically exact, leaving a few odd seconds to accumulate which amount to about one day in a century. If no change had been made until 1930, the difference would have been thirteen days. It is important, therefore, to know when the reform was adopted in various countries.

The Roman Catholic nations were very prompt in adopting the change on the date fixed or within a few years. Protestant countries declined to follow any papal mandate, most of them holding back for more than a century and thus causing great inconvenience and even riotous conflicts between neighboring communities. Protestant Germany gave way in 1700, but England remained obstinate until 1752. Russia stayed out altogether. By the same act of Parliament England abandoned the twenty-fifth of March as the beginning of the year and ordered that the day after December 31, 1751, should be January 1, 1752, with the peculiar consequence that there are no legal documents having dates between January 1 and March 24, 1751, as would have been the case had the old system remained, with the year ending on March 24. To adjust the calendar to the Gregorian year, September 3, 1752, was called September 14.

This change gave rise to phrases which are frequently encountered in the literature of the eighteenth century. To bridge over from the old custom, dates were written double and called Old Style and New Style. Unfortunately the distinction was not always made, and one is obliged to make sure which calendar the writer is using. Even in modern works, say on the period of Charles I, it is well to inquire at once whether the author has systematically translated the dates into new style, while manuscripts after 1752 may for a long time require close scrutiny. This coincides with the duty of noting the change of the beginning of the year from March to

January, already mentioned in another connection.

There follows a list of European countries with the years in which they adopted the new style.

```
        Bohemia ........................1582
        Denmark .......................1582
        France .........................1582
        Germany,
            Catholic ...................1584
            Protestant .................1700
        Great Britain ..................1752
        Holland and most of Netherlands ....1582
        Utrecht and rest of Netherlands ......1700
        Hungary .......................1587
        Ireland .......................1752
        Italy (greater part) .............1582
        Lorraine .......................1582
        Poland ........................1586
        Portugal ......................1582
        Spain .........................1582
        Strasbourg ....................1682
        Sweden ........................1753
        Switzerland,
            Catholic ................1583, 1584
            Protestant .................1700
        Tuscany ...................1749, 1751
```

The revision of the calendar made by the government of France during the Revolution proved to be temporary and local in application, but students of the contemporary documents and French literature will need to acquaint themselves with its peculiarities. A new era was decreed to begin with the abolition of monarchy, September 22, 1792, being made the first day of Year I of the French Republic. The year was divided into twelve months of thirty days each, but instead of weeks the months contained three "decades" of ten days each, while the day contained ten hours of one hundred minutes each. The pagan names of the days were abolished in favor of numbers which began with *primidi, duodi,* etc., up to *decadi,* the eleventh beginning again with *primidi.* The first nine days were called "before *decadi,*" the second nine "after *decadi* I," and the others "after *decadi* II." To make up the full year, five days were added to the end to be used as holidays and dedicated to Virtue, Genius, Labor, Opinion, and Rewards respectively. Fortunately for holiday-making these occurred between September 17 and 21, except in leap-years, when they began with the sixteenth and ended with a *Jour de la Révolution.*

The months were given names indicative of the seasons, such as *Vendémiaire* ("vintage month," September-October), *Frimaire* ("sleety month"), and *Florial* ("flowery month"). Some of these have become familiar because attached to an important event like the republican *coup d'état* on the 18th Fructidor, or Napoleon's seizure of power on the 18th Brumaire, but the chances are that one will not remember the corresponding calendar date. A comparative table is the safest and most convenient guide.

This attempt by the leaders of the Revolution to bury the past under a combination of sentiment, Greek chronology, and the metric system was in operation about a dozen years. Public documents and newspapers bear these dates, but the extent of the popular use of the system is doubtful. Not only did old habit have to be overcome, but the inconvenience of a different dating system for one lone country must have been great. This was recognized in the reign of Napoleon, and the Gregorian calendar was restored by a law taking effect on January 1, 1806.

VI

THE SEAL

The use of seals for identifying a document or for closing a communication goes back to remote antiquity. Egypt and Babylonia knew the art, for the hieroglyphic marks and the instruments themselves have been found in abundance in their ruins. The Romans likewise employed seals to protect the contents of important messages, but the study of the ancient usage lies in the province of the respective branches of archæology, and we are concerned here with the practice of the middle ages and modern times.

The seal has been a subject of profound research on the part of historical scholars because of two important questions which arise, namely, the authenticity of the document and its legal significance. With the lapse of time the establishment of a legal right may have lost its vitality, but the statements made in the document are of value only when the piece is genuine, and the seal is an important part of the evidence. Hence the care taken to preserve surviving specimens, to describe the materials, dimensions, method of attachment, inscriptions, and heraldic signs, and to define the usages of sovereigns or the various departments of government. These matters have been classified with much refinement by experts, but they can be treated here only in general outline.

Just when dignitaries of the middle ages began to use seals is not certain, but the earliest surviving documents date from the Merovingian period. The seal itself may have perished, but the mention of it or the marks on the parchment show that it was once present. Used at first only by sovereigns or persons in high authority, the importance of the seal alongside of the signature grew to a point in Carolingian times when the seal was more significant than the sign-manual. In the thirteenth century the seal was sometimes spoken of as if it were the signature itself, and later on cases might be cited where the seal alone was considered sufficient.

The practice of making duplicate copies of documents and agreements is of long standing. From early times the matter was written twice on the same sheet of parchment with a space between in which a word like *chirographum* was written in large characters. The document was then cut in two by a wavy line through this word, so that when the duplicates were compared the cut and the letters of the word must exactly fit. This saw-toothed partition is an "indenture" and gave to the agreement itself a name which survives to the present day. Modern documents can be found everywhere which begin "THIS INDENTURE SHOWETH," and derivatives are in common use, as when we read in colonial history of "indentured servants," who were working under contract for terms of years. This plan of duplication had obvious disadvantages when one copy was lost and there were no other means of proving the genuineness of the other. Hence the importance of the seal, which was used either with or without the indenture and which in governmental transactions developed a technique which affects the interpretation of documents.

From the beginning until modern times the materials of seals have been either metal or wax until the arrival of the die press, which makes an impression upon the paper itself. Lead has been continuously attached to papal documents through all these centuries, with the result that the seal, which resembled a Roman child's amulet or *bulla,* has given the name *bull* to the instrument also. Incidentally the type and inscription of papal seals have retained their primitive forms. Lead was also used by various early kings and bishops, but their dates rarely extend beyond the eleventh century.

Seals of gold were occasionally attached to documents of the highest importance, some of which have received the name Golden Bull because of their monumental significance. Usually these were not solid but were made of two thin plates soldered together and protected by a round box of wood. The use of gold for this purpose in western Europe appeared first among the Carolingians and continued to the beginning of the sixteenth century.

Wax was the material commonly used throughout the middle ages, and its use still survives. At first this was pure beeswax, but later this was often mixed with flour, linseed oil, turpentine, or pitch, and colors of various kinds came into use. Choice of color seems to have been optional at first, but in the Holy Roman Empire in the fifteenth century red could be used only by imperial grant, as this tint had become a royal monopoly. This, however, was not a general European practice.

The method of attachment of seals has some significance in determining the period of a document, but is in any case corroboratory evidence only. At first the wax was placed directly on the parchment to adhere as best it could. Later its attachment was made more certain by cutting a hole or cross slits, so that the material was secured on both sides. As seals became larger there followed greater liability of damage to the parchment and the attachment of the seals of numerous witnesses became more difficult. Hence arose the custom of fastening the wax to strips of parchment or cords. At first these strips were a part of the document, being made by a horizontal cut part way across the parchment near the bottom. This practice had its inconveniences with

the risk of tearing loose, so there followed the plan
of attaching the seal to separate slips or strings,
which were threaded into the document. To make
the attachment still stronger a fold was turned up
at the bottom, and this form became the universal
practice. The various methods of attachment have
been minutely studied by experts in sphragistics.
There were no general rules about the use of strips
or the substance or colors of cords or threads, all
depending on the taste and fancy of the various
chanceries; but when the habits of a given office or
official have been analyzed, the investigator has a
clue by which he may with other data test the authenticity of the document. This clue may be particularly valuable when only fragments remain. So
extensive is the amount of special information on
this subject that only reference to it can be made
here, with the comment that these apparently trifling matters may be important in the study of a
doubtful manuscript.

There was no rule regulating the form of a seal.
Down to the middle of the twelfth century they
were round or oval, but later many different shapes
were employed. Pointed oval, shield form, and even
fanciful shapes like the heart, triangle, lozenge,
clover-leaf, and cross are to be found. Class distinctions were not specially observed in the use of these
forms, but in the course of time it became the practice of ecclesiastics to employ the pointed oval, and

this was often followed by women of distinction, as the shape permitted the impression of a standing or seated figure. The feudal nobility used appropriately the shield form, or eventually the round seal, which could display an equestrian figure. Among the laity in general there was the widest variety both in the forms and the emblems employed, because the importance of the seal in evidence made it necessary for every man to be identified by his own.

Since the act of sealing a document was so singularly important in the establishment of legal rights, great care was exercised in the guardianship of the instruments used for the impression. States or municipalities entrusted their seals to particular officials, and sometimes the instruments were made in separable parts, each section being assigned to a special officer so that the impression could not be made unless all were present. On the death of the owner of the seal, especially in the case of sovereigns or persons in high position, the instrument was destroyed, and consequently these relics are comparatively scarce.

The danger of misuse or counterfeiting was keenly appreciated, and examples of such frauds have survived. Not only were forgeries practised, but genuine seals were removed from proper documents and attached to false ones. Corrupt officials could be induced to use the seal for private gain, and their evil doings have not always been discovered. Hence the attention demanded of the historian who for certain cases must be convinced of the legality of the document or, if it is a forgery, must discriminate between the historical statements there made. A forgery in its day and generation may have been accepted as genuine with all its lawful consequences. For all these reasons the materials, forms, and other particulars have been studied and classified by the experts.

When the wax was made to adhere directly to the parchment there could be but one imprint, but when pendant seals came into use it was possible to give them a double impression, and this led to practices which require further attention. The great seals of sovereigns may have shown two emblems of the same size, but many others had a smaller type on the reverse. This inner seal, usually called the *secretum,* was either the guarantee of the other impression or the mark of the official who confirmed its proper use. No two governments followed the same rule in the use of the second seal. Bishops as well as kings had their private official marks, and no general system can be formulated. The study of the emblems on the seals must be accompanied by thorough comprehension of the offices and departmental duties of that government. Upon this knowledge depend both determination of the honesty of the document and the interpretation of its contents. In legal or constitutional questions this study is particularly essential, and here again is an exemplification of the un-escapable fact that the reading of documents or seals is only the beginning. The powers and duties of the issuing officials must be understood. This is emphasized in all works on diplomatics, especially in Mr. Hubert Hall's *Studies in English Official Documents,* where the British system is historically analyzed.

VII

HERALDRY

To the investigator of historical materials a knowledge of heraldry is important because its emblems appear not only on the seals we have just considered but also in miniatures, engravings, or descriptions where the identity of the owner or author must be determined. Coats of arms at present seem to be trifling elegancies, for they no longer have any legal value, nor do they indicate social distinctions. They are likely to-day to excite ridicule because of their place among the ambitions of newly rich society climbers, but there was a time when heraldy was a real institution with legal privileges and an essential feature of feudal society. Because of its aspects as a factor in medieval culture and its special application to historical documents it commands a place in training for research.

The use of emblems on shields or banners is of high antiquity, but the development of armorial bearings into a system appeared first in the middle ages. The figures on the commander's military standard or on the warrior's shield became identified with his person, and eventually these emblems became heredi-

tary and acquired legal privilege and protection.
The question as to when this condition was reached
has had various answers, but it seems to be well
settled that there was no systematic heraldry before
the Norman Conquest. The Bayeux tapestry, a pic-
tured contemporary account of this expedition, shows
no regularity in the emblems of the same leaders.
Just when distinctive coats of arms were decisively
adopted is uncertain, but great influence is attributed
to the crusades which followed shortly after the Conquest. The assembly of military groups from many
countries demanded marks of distinction so that men
might know their own contingents. Identification of
leaders probably came later, and to this the adoption of the closed helmet gave an impetus because
the face of enemy or friend could not be seen. However this may have been there is no evidence for
systematic heraldry previous to the twelfth century,
and thus we have a starting point in the study of seals.
The earliest surviving seal bearing a heraldic device
is that of Robert de Chartres in 1193, and from then
onward the custom expanded till every knight and
gentleman had his own coat of arms.

Primarily this was a token of nobility, a sign that
the bearer belonged to the class which was expected
to bear actual arms in warfare. Modern writers on
heraldry have laid down two qualifications for a true
coat of arms: first, that it must be connected with
armor and second, that it must be hereditary. Yet

the medieval conception of feudalism permitted the creation of an artificial nobility which performed only civil duties and included ministers of state, judges, and other high functionaries, together with princes of the church and possibly important citizens of towns. These all held tightly to their distinctions of rank and the privileges of arms.

Eventually corporations of all kinds adopted not only seals but emblems of their own. Monastic orders, cities, gilds, and similar combinations of various descriptions were known by their peculiar devices, which cannot always be classed as heraldic but are described in heraldic terminology. So it went on downward through the social classes to the housemarks of the tradesman, where heraldry disappears. From haphazard adoption of emblems the matter grew into a jealously guarded system presided over by royal officials or a College of Arms. The numerous commissions of inquiry into titles of nobility in England demanded also proof of the right to a coat of arms. The assumption of both privileges was frequent all over Europe, for they carried not only social distinction but exemption from various taxes and duties.

Heraldic experts of the middle ages, like some of their modern successors, could invent fabulous genealogies for aspiring clients, but this need not distract the attention of the historical investigator from the fact that his duty is to determine whether the device on the seal is one properly used at the moment of its impression. This branch of information provides one more means of determining the authenticity of a document, for it often happens that other items are missing. Signatures or the inscriptions on the seals may be defaced or illegible, but the heraldic emblems may give a clue to the persons involved. Here the numerous reference books on heraldry and genealogy, with their descriptions and plates, come into very practical use.

Heraldry employs an artificial vocabulary which was created by the professional heralds during the period when the art was at the height of its importance. The terms used, mostly of French origin, have one decided advantage: they are practically the same for all the nations of western Europe. There were many different manifestations of taste in ornamentation, but the divisions of the shield and the use and names of the twelve "tinctures," metals, colors or furs, and other items are similar.

An acquaintance with the vocabulary is decidedly important when the investigator encounters in a poem or battle story a description of a coat of arms instead of an impression on a seal, or a picture with which comparison can be made. The manuals and dictionaries of heraldry give assistance, and quantities of illustrations have been printed in the genealogical records of different countries. However extensive these compilations may be, they are limited in scope to the classes which were entitled to bear arms, a situation which varied from one age to another. Hence in tracing an emblem one may come to the border line where the bearer may be properly using a seal but does not possess a registered coat of arms. As we approach modern times the quantity of private seals used by lesser individuals becomes enormous. On this account the great printed catalogue of the seal collection in the British Museum is limited to royal, ecclesiastical, corporate, and feudal nobility specimens. A comprehensive list of surviving relics of the more humble private seals would demand untold time and labor. As things now stand there are vast amounts of private documents for which the seal and its emblems are not the most important means of identification, yet quantities of problems remain.

Heraldry as an instrument in historical investigation is but one side of the subject. As one phase of medieval culture, it plays a large part in the solidification of families as well as a line of demarcation between classes. Starting from the necessities of warfare, it was made into a science for the mimic battle of the tournament and became the fount of cherished emblems of valiant deeds, the outward marks of the peculiar medieval spirit. Aside from its technical uses, it cannot be ignored in the study of social ideas and institutions.

VIII

WEIGHTS, MEASURES, AND MONEY

An essay at this point on the history of commercial calculations would be out of place, but a discussion of a few general principles will assist in holding the perspective of those useful arts, and clarify some of the particular usages encountered. Of these generalities the most striking is the extreme antiquity of weights and measures, for the use of them was evidently old at the beginning of written history and all of the ancient civilizations had well-developed systems. Second, and even more important, is the fact that there has been a consistent evolution from these ancient systems and that we have inherited and use numerous measures and terms, sometimes modified and sometimes unimpaired by the wear of millenniums. In spite of the multiplicity of languages, the various branches of the human race have followed closely the same path in formulating rules and quantities for their barters and sales.

This general uniformity speaks loudly for the commercial contacts of the civilized nations since the beginning of history, but it by no means follows that the actual measures employed were so precisely alike that one could be used for another. Local custom made differences which make necessary both translation from one language to another and calculation of comparative quantities. For this purpose tables of weights and measures are available all through history from Babylon to Britain, so that one may realize the size of the customary transactions in wheat or oil or ascertain the unit of weight in metals.

As to the price of a measure of wheat or a jar of oil there are many notices from antiquity, and these mount up in masses as the middle ages proceed. The money tokens which become more and more the medium of exchange call out other sets of tables, and one can readily find the names and the fractions of the coins of any nation and be led into the interesting study of coin emblems and numismatic art. But a statement that a *sextarius* of oil was sold for an *obolus* in Rome or that in England a quarter of wheat could be bought for eight shillings is only the first step toward an understanding of the values of those products. There must be some measure which will show by comparison what they were worth to human beings.

For this purpose various standards have been proposed. The minimum quantity of wheat necessary for human diet has been estimated and the cost calculated from prices at various periods. This might work out theoretically, but since household accounts among the poorer classes were extremely rare in the middle ages, or at any other time, the price of wheat is indefinite help, although it makes an impression when we see it soar in times of famine.

Mr. Thorold Rogers in his *History of Agriculture and Prices* reduced original items found in records and account rolls to grains of silver in order to obtain as much uniformity as possible for his comparative tables. This method has its uses but when used alone it fails to give uniform results, for silver is itself a commodity which has varied in value and it would not serve for comparison with modern wages and prices in gold-standard countries.

More helpful is the study of what an income will buy at the period in question. We use this plan every day in our own affairs and are continually recalling how cheap things used to be. Some can remember when beefsteak was twelve cents a pound and the cook received two dollars and a half a week, forgetting the general advances in income in measures of nominal dollars and cents. When we read that manual labor in England at a certain period received one and one-half pence, and harvest hands two pence, a day, wages seem very minute. When we note further that hens were priced at two pence each and eggs at one penny for two dozen, the situation seems better till one reflects that a day's common labor would not buy a hen, and twenty-four eggs would take nearly the whole of it. Rent prices vary so much according to the value of the property that they give little help. Cottages on the same manor may pay five shillings a year each when one has an acre of ground and the other none.

Numerous other items as to the cost of living may be derived from medieval accounts and from these certain aspects of economic life are visible, but any conclusion as to whether the ordinary man was better off then than now is taken at your peril. Because of the relation between wages and prices, parts of the fourteenth and fifteenth centuries have been called the happiest period for the working classes, but any estimate of that situation should include not only prices of food and cloth but also the conditions which made life worth living. Twentieth century ideals and requirements must be disregarded, but we should consider the possibilities for education, spiritual uplift, personal advancement, and other higher things open to these classes at the same time.

The study of social conditions is fascinating. The more one delves into social habits and learns of the customary life of peasants, artisans, merchants, judges, and overlords, the more realistic does history become. In the presence of the actual records, account books, or diaries of the doings of these people we walk the streets with them familiarly. We observe that the peasant lives on a limited range of diet but consumes a large amount of it, along with quantities of ale. When he is drafted into the army, he is a formidable soldier who carries a quiver of

93

arrows that is "a very sepulchre." The middle class of merchants and tradesmen is more comfortably housed but has a life circle which seems now very limited; yet somehow they built and fortified cities and adorned them with marvelous cathedrals. Princes had few conveniences, but they and their lawyers developed governments and courts which interpreted law with astonishing precision.

The repulsive crudeness seen in earlier ages makes it seem that the world has in general improved, but when it comes to specific comparisons the student is advised to proceed with care. The relative conditions of the various classes at the time can be profitably worked out and with increasing interest. To do this with precision an acquaintance with the methods of calculation used at that period is important. Whether these are simple or profound is in itself a revealing question, and for the estimation of sources they help to determine the liability to error.

To understand the difficulties and responsibilities of medieval calculations it should be remembered that for centuries these were made with Roman numerals. Arabic figures were derived from India, were known to the Arabs in the eighth century, and only gradually became known to the western world. A Latin translation of an arithmetic which appeared between 1130 and 1150 helped to spread this knowledge, but use of Arabic figures did not become general until the fifteenth century. In the meantime the use of Roman numerals went on, and they continued to be employed, especially in ecclesiastical records, long after the others were known. Stewards of estates or their clerks could manage at least a book-keeping Latin, and monastic officials were supposed to be familiar with that tongue. The house accounts of Battle Abbey, for example, were kept in Latin down to the year of dissolution. The persistence of habit and the reverence for Latin as the only permanent language may have combined to extend so long the life of this custom. The same idea of permanence sustained the use of Latin in court records, though with perhaps less hesitation in the use of Arabic numerals.

The simple additions and subtractions of a steward need not have been troublesome, since the gross income of a large estate was only a few hundreds, or at most a few thousands, of pounds. Figuring in Roman numerals, 1,536 plus 242 can be quickly solved by separating the units, tens, and hundreds in the mind.

M	D			xxx	vi
		CC		xl	ii
MD		CC		lxx	viii

Small problems of division were not more difficult. ccxxv into dcccc would be answered by saying that 200 goes into 900 four times and

25 into 100 also four times. In case of larger amounts like (M)MMMMMMCCCXX divided by CLX (16,320 ÷ 160), the reasoning would be as follows: 160 goes into 163 hundreds 100 times, leaving 320 remainder. Then, 100 would go into 300 three times, but 6 does not go into 20; so 100 goes into 200 two times, leaving 120, into which 60 also goes twice, making the result 102.

After one has worked out a few problems like this in Roman numerals while attempting to forget all his instinctive habits with Arabic figures and multiplication tables, he begins to realize why the ancients had to resort to the abacus and the counting board, with which the problems could be laid out visually by means of beads or buttons on lines representing units, tens, and hundreds. Long after Arabic numerals came into use these helps were used, not only for the benefit of the multitude who could not read but also in the counting-house and the government treasuries. Old English sheriffs brought in their accounts twice a year, laid out the amount of their collections with counters on one checker-board and their expenses on another, and took away a visible balance statement cut in notches in a slip of wood.

Robert Recorde, writing a mathematical book in 1542 in which he uses Arabic figures freely, gives also explanations as to the way the counting board should be used for the benefit of persons who cannot read. The book as reprinted with additions in 1610 still contained the instructions and diagrams for solving problems with counters. Many engravings and miniatures out of the middle ages show how continuous was the dependence upon these visible demonstrations. *Counter, counting-house,* and *exchequer* have remained imbedded in our language long after their original uses have disappeared.

When it came to extended calculations, undoubtedly the best of clerks took refuge in the counting board to verify his figures, just as the Japanese and Chinese do to-day. In this lay also a certain liability to error, for in making repeated multiplications and additions on one board the first ones would have had to be removed to make room for the next, and thus later revision of results would have been prevented. In multiplication even by the visible method a certain amount of mental arithmetic is required from one step to another. Multiplication tables came early into use, but none of these things ensured the medieval scribe against mistakes. This need not lead to general suspicion respecting early figures, but to prudent inspection such as any bookkeeping requires.

These calculators attacked a problem in multiplication in the easiest manner to explain, although to us it begins at the wrong end and requires more time to compute. Recorde lays out a diagram on the counting board to multiply 1,542 by 365. He reasons as follows, while each step is marked by moving the counters along parallel lines:

1,000 × 365	is	365,000
500 × 365 is half that		182,500
The sum of these	is	547,500
40 × 365	is	14,600
The sum of these	is	562,100
2 × 365	is	730
The final total	is	562,830

A problem which the historians of mathematics frequently produce as a sample of what the middle ages thought to be difficult is this: On a journey to Rome went seven women; each had seven mules; each mule carried seven sacks; each sack contained seven loaves; to each loaf were seven knives; each knife had seven sheaths; how many pieces are here mentioned? Laid out in Roman numerals it looks formidable for addition alone, without considering the multiplications involved. With Arabic figures it proceeds rapidly.

vii	7
xlix	49
cccxliii	343
MMCCCCi	2,401
(M)MMMMMMDCCCvii	16,807
((M))(M)MMMMMMMDCxlix	117,649
Summa . . . ((M))(M)(M)(M)MMMMMMMCCLVI .	137,256

We have little or nothing from which to estimate the rapidity with which the medieval accountant could make his calculations, unless it be the skill displayed by the modern Chinaman or Japanese in the use of his counting board. Nor can we say how

much mental arithmetic he could use with large multiplications, but doubtless familiar use of the counter
made things move more quickly than seems possible
to the modern student when he attempts to learn the
process. When one reads the accounts of the cellarer
of a monastery, for instance, where the items are
not arranged in columns but consecutively in paragraphs, it can well be assumed that the calculations
have all been worked out in advance before they
were committed to parchment. The process is not
revealed, but when so many calves or loads of
wood are sold for such a price it is well to test the
scribe here and there as to his ability in arithmetic.

That accounts were sometimes audited by outside
inspectors is indicated by marginal marks which followed an understood system. This was an arrangement of dots which showed amounts by position.
Dots on the line or below were units, those above to
the right were fives, above to the left were tens. An
illustration from Recorde shows how £198.19 s.11 d.
would appear in an auditor's notation:

```
       .            .  .           .  .              .
      . . .        . . .          . . .            . . .
       .                           .                . .
   9  score         18             19               11
```

With pence the dot to the right above stands for 6.

The coins used in trade are among the most valuable relics of historical material, although of dimin-

ishing importance as we enter modern periods. The right to issue money is an attribute of sovereignty which is now national. Every state, whether large or small, takes pride in stamping its own coins, and although the value may be the same as or similar to that of the coins of surrounding nations, the local names *franc, lira, drachma, zloty,* etc., are inevitably adopted. In ancient and medieval times this sovereign right was held by small units of government, so that cities and even smaller districts could and did issue their own currency. To this situation the coins themselves give eloquent testimony, and as historical material they form a mass more complete and sequential than any other class of relics.

Gold and silver were doubtless objects of barter in remote antiquity. The point at which pieces were stamped with a mark to show that they had been weighed was the crude beginning of coinage, and we may be certain that a considerable commerce was demanding a more convenient medium of exchange. Strong evidence points to Lydia in Asia Minor as the earliest known place of issue of coins. From its rude pellets of silver alloy there developed in the course of centuries a line of Greek moneys exhibiting the most beautiful types ever produced and of surpassing historical importance.

For the history of artistic culture Greek coins present a connected train of evidence far more complete than architecture, while at the same time they furnish a key to the standards of weight then in use. For political data they indicate the multitude of sovereign civic units which had the right to coin money —some indeed whose existence would be unknown except for coins which have been discovered. Political alliances, with joint coinage, are also confirmed by the monetary relics, while the tutelary deities honored in various places are named or portrayed with unfailing regularity. Thus through study of the spread of cults the colonies of these states can often be identified and confirmation added to the chronicles. The pictorial representations of natural objects and implements are of interest, both from a religious and a secular point of view, and an occasional fragment of architecture may give the key to an archæological problem.

The dates of Greek coins are never given in words or figures, but are determined by the names of the rulers, city officials, mint-masters, or engravers which may be included. Portraits of rulers begin only at a late date, for the heads are always deities or mythological heroes. Even Alexander the Great did not break this tradition, for his noble head is adorned with the lion-skin of Hercules or the horns of Jupiter Ammon. One of his successors omitted such attributes, and thus the long history of sovereigns' portraits began. The value of these as historical material in evidence of character depends upon the state of contemporary art.

101

The high artistic value of Greek coins was due to the advanced state of taste and skill which prevailed in other branches of art and to the fact that the engraver was not limited as to the depth of relief. Coins nowadays are made to be laid up in piles, and consequently the relief must be flat, but there was no such restraint upon the ancient artist. While the risk of abrasion was unfortunately greater, the product of the die was much finer.

Any estimate of the amount of coin in circulation during a given period must consider the mechanical process of fabrication, which for thousands of years was extremely primitive. Throughout ancient and medieval history coins were struck off one at a time with a hammer and dies in a multitude of simple workshops. A screw press giving greater regularity, but probably only a little more speed, came into use in the sixteenth century, while the power press had to wait till the nineteenth. Information as to the quantity of coins required in trade or stored in treasuries during the early centuries is rare and uncertain, and hence the light reflected upon history by coinage is preponderantly artistic and political. Roman art declined from the Greek, and the coinage of the middle ages fell into a mire from which it took centuries to escape, but the survival of hundreds of types from the mints of medieval monarchs, bishops, princes, cities, and lordships, great and small, testify eloquently to the multiplex subdivisions of sovereignty and confirm the records which become increasingly abundant respecting the issue and withdrawal of coins, the persons who were entitled to strike them and the punishment of counterfeiting. Lordships did not scruple to debase the metal, but the counterfeiter risked the loss of a hand.

In modern history the actual coins are of less significance because we are furnished in other ways with information as to their metallic content, the limits of legal circulation, and their exchange value. We are told in words of the ill effects of debasement and the reforms of an Elizabeth, while records of prices and the credit of governments become more important than the metal medium of exchange.

In the study of ancient and medieval coinage we have to do with relics which are eloquent with the tale of social, economic, and political custom. Mechanical processes, weights and measures, artistic conditions, emblems of mythology, historical pictures, ruling personages, units of government, and spread of commerce are all revealed in these metallic tokens.

IX

GENEALOGY

There are good reasons for the study of genealogy besides family pride or the desire to join a
patriotic society. The property rights and posses-
sions of historical characters have depended upon
descent, and courts of law have given the question
the most careful consideration. When certain offices
were hereditary it was necessary for this reason also
to have the title legitimate and clear. Seats in aris-
tocratic senates and in all houses of lords have depended, not only on the writs of summons, but on
the family history of the occupants as well. During
certain periods army offices were given only to men
of high birth, and social distinctions have sometimes
required the display of at least three generations of
distinguished family title with the corresponding
coats of arms. These and numerous other conditions
make it necessary at times for the historical student to follow a family line and ascertain the truth
about what we may call the external situation of one
of its members.

The discredit which has fallen upon this pursuit
has been due to the extravagant claims of ancient

descent which have been put forward, based upon pride or assumption or forgery, not to speak of modern social ambitions. Ancient kings were alleged to have descended from the gods even when this involved scandalous relations not to be tolerated in good society. That claims of similar derivation were made for primitive European rulers is understandable, since high origin was the foundation of their authority. Later, after gods were discarded, the tracing of a long descent remained a matter of pride or necessity.

Among early Germanic peoples relationship was important so long as they lived under the laws which required the family to be responsible for the crimes of its members. It was a matter of decided interest to know whether you were obliged to contribute to the fine of a poor relative, or whether you were near enough to the family of a victim to receive a portion of the compensation. The primitive Welsh had similar codes, and the fondness for relationships still ascribed to them may be an inheritance from a time when such matters were jealously remembered. Heroic actions and many other matters have helped to preserve family history and incidentally have tempted men to claim distinguished connections without warrant.

Medieval English kings occasionally instituted proceedings of inquiry to ascertain "by what warrant" the gentry of the country were holding titles, privileges, and lands, while the College of Arms preserved the records, not always perfect, of the genealogies of the upper classes. Under the Ancient Régime in France the nobility enjoyed so many privileges and exemptions from taxes that quantities of aspiring families assumed or invented connections to which they were not entitled. The great finance minister Colbert cut a wide swath through this growth of weeds by means of his investigating commissions, much to the benefit of the royal treasury. All along there have been among heralds and professional genealogists those who satisfied their clients with long pedigrees based on similarity of names or invented descent, and all together these perversions have thrown a shadow of suspicion over an honorable branch of knowledge.

Although this interest in family lineage goes back to primitive peoples and conditions, the systematic recording of descent in formal records is of comparatively late origin. In English history it appears with the general adoption of surnames and the rise of heraldry. For the beginnings of these one may go back to the twelfth century, but the development was slow and records are so doubtful that very few families can be traced to the Norman Conquest. The experts say that for the majority of English lines the fifteenth and sixteenth centuries are the extreme limits. The establishment of the College of Heralds in 1484 gave an official recognition to genealogical recording which has since developed from tabular pedigrees into elaborate family histories.

To the student of the social sciences there are several important phases of genealogy for consideration. Naturally the first is to establish the true line of descent by documentary evidence. Based upon this will be the study of personal characteristics and the qualities of mind which are prominent in that family and which appear to have been inherited by the individual whose biography is being written. Not all physical features are of the first importance. Whether the family is marked by red hair or blue eyes may be left, from the social point of view, to the operation of the Mendelian law, but a strong bodily frame and a tendency to long life, or the opposite qualities, may be highly significant, especially among ruling classes. The peculiar Hapsburg face, persisting for some seven centuries till it appears in the latest king of Spain, is an item in the evidence of descent, but less interesting than the qualities of mind and body displayed by that family. Long life and long reigns appearing from time to time among rulers of France and England have had a marked social effect, whether vigorous or weak, because of the continuity of a single policy. Genealogy may assist in the explanation of such situations, but too often this help is not called in unless the ruler is actually insane.

Normal conditions require this study of personality and inheritance, but it must be said that for ancient and early modern history the general evidence is scarce and inadequate. Only for the most prominent characters are such descriptions available. Certain items of parentage and environment may be obtained, and an author's writings may disclose his powers of mind, but for origins of his qualities we are left much in the dark.

Data for family history from the past two centuries are more satisfactory, and the characteristics inherited by a biographical subject can be more easily traced. It is possible in many cases to trace the source of particular traits or natural qualities. Francis Galton has shown that genius may run in families, and this is likewise true of less phenomenal characteristics. Physical stamina alone is an important item, even if intellectual inheritance cannot be so well determined.

The principal object of a biographical study, of course, is to show what use the subject made of his inherited or acquired powers, and the stress upon family traits can be overdone. Much sentimental slush has been written about parental influence where more restrained statements would have given a convincing picture. The emotions awakened by family ties are among the most precious in our civilization and require due consideration, but the investigator of inherited qualities should remain calm and objective in their presence. What ancestors can really do is to provide a physical basis, a human bodily construction which the descendant may use or misuse. Parental training and family influence are most important, but they belong in another class of questions.

The tracing of descent and the writing of family histories has become more than ever an occupation of amateurs and experts. Printed compilations of pedigrees abound, and in the older countries these are likely to be concerned with the upper classes of society. Genealogical accounts of American families have multiplied to an enormous extent, but however important these may be in starting an inquiry they should not be regarded as infallible. Errors or hasty conclusions may occur anywhere along the line, and the writer of a family history should make sure that a descent is proved from point to point by documentary evidence.

The many sources for this kind of history are not always obvious to the beginner, consequently one or more of the guide-books for genealogical study should be consulted. A start can well be made by consulting a list of published genealogies, of which several are available for England and America, giving references to books and shorter articles. For an English family history the amount of printed material appears at first sight to be infinite and bewildering. However, when a place of abode or a topographical area has been established, the finding of the relations and activities of the persons becomes a matter of patience and assiduity. Within the last century parish records have been published in great numbers, although the list is not complete. These were made obligatory under Henry VIII, and with many breaks and deficiencies have persisted to the present time. They show births, marriages, and deaths, with parish activities which may reveal the names of persons sought. The records of town councils were kept for business purposes only, but the names of officials and other people concerned may add items desired.

The publications of the British Public Record Office are too numerous to be cited here. They consist chiefly of indexes and careful calendars of documents derived from every department of government, with some lists from outside sources. In some cases it is obvious that genealogical material is to be found, but it is not so clear that a Pipe Roll of the Exchequer, for example, or the minutes of the Privy Council will contain anything wanted for that purpose. Here is where the book of the genealogical expert will suggest a resort to sources not dreamed of by the beginner.

The manuscript sources for English history are unique in their abundance and continuity. For legal and social purposes heraldic records were officially maintained, and while these may contain errors they served the purpose of establishing pedigrees and evidence of property rights conditioned on descent. Much of this material has been worked into the later books on genealogy.

Court records are of high importance in all fields of historical research, and much has been done to facilitate the examination of the English material, both printed and manuscript. The Chancery was often called upon to establish relationships in the settlement of estates, but personal items are found in the pleas of the King's Bench, the Court of Common Pleas, the Court of the Exchequer, and all down the line. Here also the genealogical guides will lead the beginner into unsuspected sources of information. The records of the universities, the medical and legal professions, and the army and navy all have their places in such research.

Until the middle of the nineteenth century English wills were deposited in ecclesiastical courts extending from the archbishoprics of Canterbury and York to the various bishoprics and certain minor courts within these. In 1858 this function was transferred to civil courts of probate centered in London at Somerset House with districts throughout the country. The older diocesan records are for the most part deposited in the corresponding modern district court, where under certain regulations they may be examined.

Testamentary documents have long been recognized as most important among genealogical materials. The difficult problem is to find the place where they were deposited or copied. In America the early wills were recorded in small places owing to the fact that settlements were scattered. In New England, for example, wills were for a long time incorporated in the minutes of the town meetings along with property transactions and other matters. Some of these towns have since been included in large cities, and it may take time to discover where the old records have been deposited.

The printing of early wills and parish records goes on with great vigor, and these afford much help when the investigator is sure of the locality where his subject lived. To pursue an individual through a multitude of local records is not only wearisome but likely to be futile, because of the similarity of Christian names and the quantity of families bearing the same ordinary surnames. It may take time and other sources to establish the place of residence, but it will be economy in the end to do it first. Difficulty is added by a marked independence in the spelling of names characteristic of our early settlers. A tendency to phonetic rendering with duplication of consonants and chronic interchange of *i* and *y* is clearly visible, but these peculiarities soon become familiar, like the long *f* for *s*.

As already indicated, the materials for genealogical study range promiscuously from tombstones to cabinet councils, from parish registers to parliamentary records. As to the form in which the gleanings from these sources should be published there is diversity of opinion, but one thing is certain, namely, that the arrangement should be so marked or numbered that the direct descent is clear, with collateral branches, however interesting, placed where they do not interfere with this design. Models for comparison can readily be found.

The establishment of a family pedigree is a matter of legitimate pride, but the publication could be more useful to the world if the personal characteristics of the figures in it were included. The amount of material is usually so extensive that the treatment does not get much beyond the style of the Scriptures, in which we are told that "Isaac begat Jacob." Further details may (or may not) be found in biographical dictionaries, but the student of the social sciences must ordinarily content himself with the heritage which his subject has received from one or two previous generations. In the cases of sovereigns and statesmen and a few degenerate families there are exceptions to this situation, but a wide field is left open for the study of personality.

X

DIPLOMACY

The international relations of the world have been embodied in a variety of materials which, because of their connection with diplomacy, have been classified as diplomatic documents. Ambassadors between nations have been employed since the beginnings of history, but the mass of material which has accumulated since the middle ages has now become so overwhelming that no man attempts to master it as a whole. Indeed, in modern times the amount of documents which covers only a short period has become so great that the investigator must select only certain ones for close study and in particular must be aware of the weight and value of those which he selects. It is for these reasons that a few words are introduced here concerning the nature of diplomatic documents.

For centuries this class of material has been looked upon with suspicion. The conception of an ambassador was that he was sent abroad to deceive the rulers of the other nation. His principal business was to advance the cause of his own nationality or his own sovereign, and in order to do so he might use any form of prevarication which would serve this purpose. It is not difficult to prove that deception was used, and consequently communications between nations were justly suspected of falsehood or at least of concealing the truth. This does not permit us to reject the study of these documents, for it is important to know what methods were employed. Other materials may not necessarily come under this suspicion. Communications between the home government and its ambassadors are likely to contain the truth, and the greater part of diplomatic documents are included in this class. Instances may occasionally occur where a government will deceive its own envoy, but this is not the rule, for the correspondence between them will usually show the motives and objects of the foreign ministry. It is the duty of the investigator not only to note the motive behind a diplomatic transaction but also the means employed to attain that end.

International business in modern times is conducted according to strict rules of etiquette and procedure. These forms have gradually grown into an accepted code since the beginning of the eighteenth century, but it by no means follows that earlier documents were presented without form or lack of precedent in the chanceries from which they emanated. Modern practice has grown out of the experience of centuries. While some of its formalities seem somewhat artificial, yet the presence of a code makes clear the meaning of every act and removes the danger of misunderstanding. It is, therefore, the duty of the investigator to consider carefully not only the words of the document but also the source from which it comes and the weight commonly given to a paper of that class.

According to present practice a foreign ambassador is appointed only after the foreign government has been consulted as to whether the candidate is a person agreeable to it. There are probably different reasons for a favorable reply, but a refusal will probably follow when the public utterances of that person have shown a pronounced hostility to the foreign nation. This may seem at first sight an act of pride or resentment on the part of the foreign nation, but it is in fact a protection for the nation sending the ambassador. It has been an age-long precept and experience that only an envoy agreeable to the foreign state can accomplish anything for his own government.

The etiquette followed in the reception of an ambassador has become so much a matter of form that it has little significance. Having notified the Secretary of State or corresponding official of his arrival and having exhibited his letters of credence, the ambassador is given an audience with the sovereign or chief executive of the state. On this occasion he makes a brief address which has already been examined and approved by the Department of State.

This speech is inevitably a message of good-will from the ruler of his own state, and the reply is equally good-natured and replete with best wishes. The ceremony of presentation and the conducting of the ambassador back and forth to his lodgings no longer have any significance. In former times, however, the actions of the envoy on this day were sometimes worth noting. It was customary for the envoy to enter the royal city accompanied by a large body of retainers, all dressed in rich costume and provided with elaborate equipment of every kind. The object of this display was to exhibit the wealth and power of his own sovereign, with the implied hint that it would be dangerous to interfere with his plans or impinge upon his territory. It was not unusual for ambassadors in their ordinary passage through the streets to make considerable display for similar reasons. There arose also many quarrels between ambassadors, or disputes with the Department of State, respecting the order of precedence. These questions are of little significance to the historian except as they show the assumptions of that nation or perhaps the pride of that particular envoy. In modern times precedence is settled by seniority or by the alphabet or by mutual understanding, and trouble over this problem has practically disappeared.

Communications between two governments are transmitted from the office of the Secretary of State to the corresponding official in the foreign country. This takes place through the national ambassador resident at that court, and he is given instructions as to the form which this communication shall take. The two departments of state, or of foreign affairs, will have copies of this document, or possibly the receiving ministry will take minutes to show what transpired. The various kinds of communications have taken on well-defined forms which are universally known and consistently followed. The definitions of each are usually found in manuals of diplomatic procedure. It should be understood also that other conversations between the ambassador and the foreign office can take place and that no records are necessarily made of these. Little questions of no importance may arise, or it may be necessary to make appointments for meetings, and these may possibly get into the diary of the ambassador. Real business, however, between the two governments is carried on under careful instructions and the contacts may be made through the following forms.

1. The Note may be written in the first or third person, the latter being used on the more formal occasions. The document may be delivered in person by the ambassador, or at other times he may be directed to read the contents to the foreign minister. He may be ordered to leave a copy, to give a copy when asked to do so, or to refuse to comply with such a demand. In case the copy is refused, the min-

ister may decline to listen in order that he may be protected from false reports or rumors of the affair, or that at some future date he may not be compelled to depend upon his memory alone for the details of the transaction. In order to overcome formal difficulties of this kind the minister may receive a communication verbally, take his own notes, and submit a minute of the same for confirmation. Consequently, in spite of the formalities, the actual contents of the communication may get into the state papers.

2. The *Note Verbale* is written in the third person, terminating in a formula of courtesy, but is neither signed nor addressed. This form is often used to get a record of a conversation or in order to put a question. It may be a piece of serious importance, but it is not destined for publication. Although delivered in writing, it is treated as if given verbally and put on record so as not to be forgotten. Such communications are not often found in print.[1]

3. A *Mémoire,* memorial, or memorandum contains detailed statements or arguments and is essentially the same as a note; not containing date, signature, or formula of courtesy, however, it is conveniently delivered with a short covering letter. In earlier times this was called a deduction, or *exposé de motifs.*

[1] E. Satow, *Guide to Diplomatic Practice.* I, 85.

4. The *Note Collective* is the combined action of several or all the powers represented at one court. It amounts to an alliance of all these foreign powers to bring pressure upon one state. The tenor of such a document is sometimes friendly and sometimes severe but is not in any case likely to be received in a friendly light. The use of the collective note is comparatively rare.

5. Identical Notes, *Notes Identiques,* have been occasionally used to express an opinion or exert pressure upon a foreign government and still avoid the appearance of an alliance of powers. Such notes are not necessarily word for word identical but are in substance the same and are presented as far as possible at the same time. The manuals of diplomacy give careful directions respecting the formal parts of a note.

The proper use of titles and phrases of courtesy is essential to the conduct of good business, yet these are not necessary for the identification or proof of the document. The dates and the names of the persons concerned are of vital importance. However, the study of complimentary phrases, especially as they developed in the seventeenth and eighteenth centuries, throws light on the interesting manners and social distinctions prevailing in that period. This exaggerated politeness is particularly marked in German documents.

6. Credentials for an ambassador are sometimes

issued in the form called *Lettres de Chancellerie*, but more often as *Lettres du Cabinet*, which are less formal. In both cases the style is exactly prescribed. These forms are also used for notices of birth or death, congratulation, or condolence.

Credentials always express the hope that the ambassador's communications will be given full credit and that the best of relations may prevail between the two countries. These are formalities of long usage and not spontaneous outbursts of feeling, although they may be true. The extent of the powers granted to the ambassador for use on his mission is exhibited in a commission which is practically a public document, for it is to be displayed whenever the question of his authority arises. Such a commission is signed by his sovereign and, except in England, is countersigned by a minister. In studying a diplomatic conference, for example, it is important to take note of the extent of power granted to the respective ambassadors, for it makes a great difference whether the envoy is authorized to conclude the business or whether he must refer all points to the home office.

The foregoing documents establish the formal and legal position of the ambassador at a foreign court. The great mine of historical information is to be found in the instructions given to the envoy and the reports which he sends back to his government. From time to time books have been written for the instruction of diplomatic agents as to how they should conduct themselves at the courts of foreign powers. These works reflect the tone of diplomatic intercourse at the time they were written, and it is an interesting study in itself to compare the instructions given in the seventeenth or eighteenth century with examples from Foster [2] or Satow,[3] writing in the twentieth century. A delightful book describing diplomatic procedure in the last quarter of the seventeenth century was written by an anonymous Spanish diplomat. He gives counsel and direction for the conduct of ambassadors and draws the faint line between truth and deception which was characteristic of diplomacy at that period.

Great numbers of examples can be found where general counsels are combined with specific instructions from the home government. For an illustration, take the instructions given by the English government to the ambassador about to go to Sweden in 1727. He is directed to seize every opportunity to assure the King of Sweden of the great satisfaction that the King of England takes in the alliances into which they have entered. He is to get all possible information from his predecessor as to the state of affairs in Sweden, particularly as to the ministers with whom he must come in contact, and as to the temper and personal characteristics of the senators and the principal personages in the governments. He

[2] J. W. Foster, *The Practice of Diplomacy.*
[3] E. Satow, *op. cit.*

must watch with all diligence the movements and intrigues of other envoys and agents resident at Stockholm and send home exact accounts of what he discovers. He must find out from his predecessor what sort of behavior the Russian minister has displayed toward him. He is to maintain good relations with the envoys of all nations who are in amity with England and particularly to cultivate the friendship of the ambassador of France. He is to become as intimate as possible with Count Horn, who has the greatest influence in all the affairs of Sweden, while at the same time he must exhibit all deference to the King without giving offense to the Count and his party. He must strive to maintain the best understanding between the King and the Count, because the success of the affairs of England depends upon the stability of that situation. With these and a few other minor instructions the English government hopes that the great Russian influence over Sweden at the time will eventually be broken.[4]

Once the ambassador reaches his place, a constant flow of instructions and reports ensues in which the policy of the home government is discoverable. Policies and plans may not succeed, but in these documents one finds the intentions of the government and the causes of changes which may take place. Reports to the home government review the

[4] *British Diplomatic Instructions,* Vol. 5, *Sweden, 1727–1789* (Camden Society, XXXIX, 1).

details of any special negotiation and possibly give the reactions of the other ambassadors to that project. If any ambassador has started a false rumor as to what his government is going to do, this is the channel by which it reaches its intended destinations. The watchful envoy will attempt to give the state of public opinion on questions liable to affect his own country. He will report the progress of laws through the legislature and forewarn against impending evil in these acts or call attention to advantages which may follow.

The classical examples of such reports are those sent home by the ambassadors of Venice in the sixteenth century. They describe in great detail the diplomatic affairs in which the ambassadors were concerned and also public events and the manners and customs of the peoples to which they were accredited. In general, however, such reports relate to political situations. A vast amount of such material has already found its way into print. Modern governments fix a limit beyond which their archives are not open to research. This is to prevent embarrassment from any untimely publicity of living issues, and consequently the investigator cannot expect to come up to date by that route. Yet a government will often publish recent documents when it seems necessary to rise to the government's own defense on a particular issue. In such cases the question arises as to whether all of the pertinent material has been made public. Sometimes such a matter has to wait a full generation before the full truth is revealed.

Still more interesting and often more valuable is the correspondence which ambassadors conduct during their periods of office. This may consist of letters written to members of the cabinet for their private perusal, or to other persons in whom the ambassador places confidence. The writer is likely to use more freedom in describing persons and situations than he would in a communication for the eyes of his sovereign or the official ears of his cabinet. Very often such semipublic papers, as well as much really public material, have been considered as private property by the receiver and consequently have not been placed in the official archives. This confusion was particularly marked in England until quite modern times, with the result that quantities of papers which properly belong in the Public Record Office will be found in family archives or public libraries. Much of this matter has been published and more will be in the future, but the investigator always has to bear in mind that archives are not necessarily complete. Of such illuminating outside material the correspondence of Lord Chesterfield with Newcastle is but one example in a multitude.

It appears then that the diplomatic material which the historian has before him consists, first, of purely formal transactions which were regulated by etiquette or by international rule; second, of the documents which were to be presented to the foreign state, sometimes formal and sometimes not, and which may or may not have been made public at the time; third, of the instructions to the ambassador and his reports, all of which were considered confidential and were liable to be kept from the public for a considerable time; and fourth, of the private correspondence of ambassadors so far as it related to the international matters they had in hand.

XI

GEOGRAPHY

The history of a people cannot be separated from the geographical environment in which it existed. This fact has become so clear to modern investigators that one might assume it as an obvious axiom, but the field of observation is so constantly widening, with new elements coming into view, that the historical student is obliged to take notice of many things which his predecessors failed to see. We are no longer satisfied with the older historical books which covered the subject of geography with a few paragraphs and a flat map of political boundaries. Peoples and nations are not abstract conceptions floating in historical space, but every one of them is, or was, planted somewhere on this solid earth. There is nowhere else to go in this life. We need not go so far as to make geography and climate the determining factors in national life, but every investigator is bound to inquire how much they explain. Studies of a short period may not escape this duty, and limited themes like the history of law, religion, or art get illumination from the environment which writers have often overlooked.

The mathematical measurement of the earth's surface is the work of the science of geodesy. The knowledge of the heights and depths and coastal outlines of the world has been of vast importance to humanity in an economic sense, while its progress is a part of the intellectual evolution of the race. The methods of geodetical calculation and the details of procedure are not under consideration here, but rather the relation of man to the earth upon which he lives. *Anthropogeographie, La Géographie Humaine,* Human Geography are the terms used by the specialists to describe this hyphenated science.

Accurate accounts of battles, whether fought in the time of Edward I or under General Grant, call for minute descriptions of the terrain upon which the contest was fought. It is decidedly important to know whether one party was advantageously stationed on high ground and whether the intervening field was smooth and open or infested with swamps and hidden pitfalls. Likewise in times of peace the topography of the land upon which a people or a community carries on its daily activities is an essential factor in its existence and its history.

The difference between mountains and plains in the matter of hay-making is at once apparent. Upon steeply slanting surfaces grass-plots a few rods square must be mowed laboriously by hand and the product carried upon the shoulders of men or women to the place of storage. On the plateau there will be more abundant crops and the use of machinery will be possible. In Norway rain and moisture is so abundant that even on level ground the hay must be hung on special fences to dry. This means a laborious process of thatching in one handful at a time which greatly increases the expenditure of time and effort and, naturally, the cost of the product. In a multitude of ways conditions of soil and climate direct the occupations of mankind, with consequences which have been often worked out from the strictly economic point of view. The effect of all these things on the civilization of the people, their cultural and intellectual life, is a further problem which has been given more scientific attention in these modern days.

One might suppose at first thought that geographical conditions would be considered chiefly in the making of general conclusions about a people or a civilization after the work of investigation has been completed. True enough, geography, environment, and nature all come into a final survey, but they belong also in the front rank of inquiry. Their influence is to be noted from point to point, and throughout the narration they form a background to the political or intellectual actions described. Historians have been slow to understand the importance of these factors, but modern writers now realize, at least in part, that environment must come in. Important works begin with a description of the country. Some of these are inadequate, but they appre-

ciate the desirability of scenery for the drama about
to be described.

Breasted's history of Egypt is an excellent modern
example. His first chapter on "The Land" is indispensable for an understanding of what follows. The
political limits of ancient Egypt, as well as the internal life of the people, were bound up in a valley
some eight hundred miles in length flanked on both
sides by a tropical desert and so occupied by the
Nile that it left only strips of arable land ten miles
in width at the very greatest. Since the country had
very limited rainfall, the population were absolutely
dependent upon the periodical floods of the Nile for
the watering of their fields. Ages of floods had produced an extremely fertile soil, and the people became expert in the employment of irrigation by the
use of simple mechanical devices. Owing to the surrounding deserts, further moated by the Red Sea,
there was only one important opening to the outer
world, namely, at the northeastern corner via the
Isthmus of Suez. Consequently the nation was long
isolated and grew up with its particular religion,
social customs, and forms of art, the splendors of
which have been revealed in modern times. The
great length of the narrow country made government difficult, which resulted in the spectacle of rival
governors and princes in frequent conflict, rendering
invasion from outside eventually possible. Thus
many things both political and social were pro-

foundly influenced by the physical situation in which the nation was planted.

The case of Egypt is so obvious that the argument is granted at once, but when it comes to countries where the contrasts in climate and physical geography are not so vividly marked, the student of history may not fully appreciate the influence of these factors. He may readily see that the mountain ridges of ancient Greece divided the country into numerous tribes which developed different ideas of language and social order and, furthermore, that these divisions were accentuated by arms of the sea which penetrated the country, tempted the inhabitants to nautical adventure, and led eventually to the spread of Greek culture over the Mediterranean basin; but when it comes to a plain, rolling country without sharp geographical individuality, the student does not always take pains to inquire about physical features.

The influence of place and climate was noticed incidentally by ancient writers, but their information was imperfect and their conclusions were sometimes fantastic. More elaborate explanations were attempted from the sixteenth century onward, but not until the nineteenth did the matter take on anything like a scientific aspect. Human geography is now a distinct branch of knowledge, having for its object the study of the relationship of the earth and its atmospheric phenomena to the human race. Distinguished scholars have devoted their talents to the investigation of the subject, and special topics in that field have called out the energies of many others.

One object of such inquiry is to find whether there are laws which govern the effect of environment upon man. The influence of coastal plains, of mountain regions, of steppes and deserts, of rivers, navigable and otherwise, and of climate on human energy and similar topics have been studied with the view of learning how much these factors determine the activities of mankind and what the human race has done to overcome difficulties in its surroundings. Environment has had effect upon the physical structure of the body as to size and color, as well as upon mental capacity. Important psychical effects are seen in the differences in religion and mythology among peoples in different physical and climatic situations. In one place hell may be thought of as a place of darkness and intense cold, while in another it is hot with eternal fire. Language, especially in the matter of vocabulary, is affected through occupations, which are primarily determined by the nature of the location.

The movements of people and their contacts with others are dependent upon facilities for transport and travel as determined by rivers, oceans, roads, and mountain passes. Recognition of this fact has led to study of the effect of migration and change of climate upon physical stamina, habits, and character.

All these influences stand out clearly in the history of primitive peoples, but as civilization becomes more complex generalizations become more difficult.

It might perhaps be assumed in these days that an investigator of a limited period or the history of a special theme would of course take note of the natural environment surrounding his subject, but there is always the risk that he will fail to see as many of these factors as he should. The multitude of strictly human questions, such as the development of laws, arts, and doctrines, may take time and space due to elements which are also economically and socially fundamental. For that reason it is essential to know what human geography has to say about the relations of mankind to the earth, if for no other reason than to see how many natural factors have played a part in history and thus obtain suggestions which may apply to the topic in hand.

Taken as a whole, human geography deals with types and general conceptions. The influences of mountains in general, of life on plains or steppes, of rivers—sometimes seen as barriers and sometimes as means of communication—of the presence or absence of building materials, and of other elements can be illustrated from actual examples and historical cases but are eventually built into a series of rules or general theories. Economists do not need to be told that these same conditions help to explain concrete cases where single nations or smaller groups are concerned. Here is where training in economic method becomes essential to the historical student. Without this preparation some of the prominent economic factors may stand out in his problem, but with the proper habits of thinking many other lines of inquiry will be suggested and sources of information pointed out which otherwise would have escaped him. The demands of history in these days are too extensive and too exacting to allow the omission of anything that explains the life and activities of the people.

The Le Play school of economists carried this matter of location down to the family budget and studied not only the landscape but also the geological structure to see if it governed occupations or means of livelihood. Climate and seasons were brought to bear on the capacity for work, and other natural conditions were used to explain the status of single family groups. The results may not have led to a permanent theory of family economics, but the method was very helpful to scientific philanthropy and the kinds of questions raised are decidedly suggestive to the investigator.

The same method was applied by this group to historical cases on a larger scale. Ancient Egypt, Babylon, and peoples less remote were subjected to a similar questionnaire and the results digested in short essays. The volumes of the *Science Sociale* contain a long list of these studies, and while later knowledge may change the conclusions, the scope of the questions employed is instructive for any period of history.

The work of Frederick J. Turner dealing with the Western Frontier set American historians on a new path. The soils and their most productive pioneer crops, the configurations of the landscape, the vicissitudes of an independent pioneer life, and other economic elements were made to give a fresh explanation of the political and social life of the advancing West. This cannot be done by reference only to ancestral traits and to the regions and institutions from which the settlers migrated. The geographical and topographical method must be applied, and the same procedure needs to be employed with other portions of American history.

Eminent European scholars, not only in the field of theoretical geography, but also in national history have made close studies of surface conditions. Karl Lamprecht, later an historian of the German people as a whole, made his early reputation with a voluminous research among agricultural names and field designations whereby the location of early Teutonic groups was established. Study of place names in Switzerland showed that a great part of these were derived from persons, and the conclusion was inevitable that they were settlements of feudal chieftains made at a time when the population was bound up in that system. Similarly the movements of the

Danes in England have been traced through their settlements, and out of geographical terms have come, not only myths, traditions, and popular obsessions, but genuine local history and the linguistic evolution of place names of to-day.

From another point of view the historian is concerned with the geographical obstacles which man has overcome. Primitive society was severely restricted by these barriers, but the conflict began early. Looking beyond the European world, we study with profound admiration the terraced hills of South America from whose sides the ancient Incas wrested their crops. These conflicts form a test of enterprise and civilization.

The history of transportation has been that of a conquest of natural obstacles in a conflict which for ages proceeded very slowly, gaining its rapid tempo only during the last hundred years. Regions of later occupation have sometimes entered quickly into the modern phase. California, for example, was difficult of access at the time of its discovery. With few harbors on its coast, it was bounded on the land side by deserts and formidable mountains. The few passes were difficult and were discovered late, and so life remained primitive till the discovery of gold in 1849. In less than a century since that time the mountains have been penetrated with smooth roads and bored with tunnels. Railroads and automobiles bring hundreds of thousands of people annually into its sunny climate, where they find that former cattle-ranges and dry areas have been watered with great irrigation systems and that electric power is moving great industries.

The whole of the comparatively short period of California's constitutional history is thus marked step by step by the conquest of geographical obstacles. These conquests are of great consequence in the social as well as the economic development of the State, and the investigator of any part of this must be sufficiently acquainted with geographic methods to estimate the social value of the struggle with nature. At the same time it need not be forgotten that here as elsewhere nature has given direction to the life of the people. The long north-and-south extent of the State presents four or more climatic divisions with consequent variety of products. The north as a whole is a well-wooded agricultural country with considerable rainfall. The Cascade Mountains along the coast protect a narrow strip from extremes of heat or cold. The San Joaquin Valley in the central interior is warm with moderate rainfall, while Southern California below the Tehachipi Mountains is the northwest corner of Central America, with a variable climate from the cool coast to the hot interior, where the extreme is found in the tropical heat of the Imperial Valley. Man enjoys the natural fruitfulness of all these regions by giving artificial application of water to a naturally rich soil and by other adaptations of geophysical conditions.

The making of maps has had a long history, and the early specimens contained much guess-work, but we are much indebted to them for indications of the state of geographical knowledge. In these days the most remote parts of the earth are getting into charts, and the civilized countries are being measured to the last decimal point for heights and depths and geological contents. These physical maps are important not only for present economic use but for an understanding of historical conditions. The present topographical atlas, or even the army map of France, can contribute much to an understanding of the French Revolution, not only in regard to the movement of military forces, but in elucidation of the economic situation as it was described by Arthur Young. Consequently it behooves the student to learn to read modern maps properly. The best of them are provided with contour lines which show elevations, and these require a proper use of the imagination to translate them into hills and valleys. One is not always assisted by shading, which may exaggerate one way or another, but a little practice will make winding lines stand out in successive levels.

XII

HISTORICAL EVIDENCE

The use of historical evidence is not a mysterious operation. It is only the constructive application of common sense to the data which the investigator has accumulated. History is a narrative of the actions of human beings in connection with the topic of research, whether it be in politics, law, religion, music, or mechanical arts. It may be necessary to have the wits sharpened by acquaintance with the general laws of psychology or of climate or of some of the natural sciences, but these are surmountable attainments which add riches to the historian's equipment for the employment of ordinary everyday logic.

It is a well-worn axiom that the more one knows about the personal habits, the social customs, the educational advantages, or even the mechanical devices of a people, the better able will he be to apprehend, not only its general history, but also the part of it which he has chosen for research. The problem lies in the fitting of the investigator's special data into the general situation, in giving true weight to each specimen of his material, and in producing a clear picture. Naturally practice and the study of the elements of this art will give greater facility than any beginner possesses.

Archæology and anthropology have accomplished wonders in finding the origins of primitive society and showing the early development of arts and social institutions; but if we desire to learn the history of political groups and the progressive conquest of the earth, the written word is indispensable. Relics of human art have been found in geological formations which date man's existence back presumably fifty thousand years or more, but this is a broad hypothesis rather than a certified date. That field of discovery will be open to change for a long time. Egyptian history is extending deeper than ever into the past, but we should still be at sea concerning when things happened without the inscriptions and literary remains which give basic testimony from which to calculate. The marvelous Mayan civilization might remain an uncharted puzzle were it not for decipherable dates on the monuments which place it within a pre-Christian era where it may be compared with European contemporaries.

An interesting study of trees as recorders of time has been made by Dr. A. E. Douglass of Arizona. Examination of the annual rings of growth has enabled him to establish not only years of moisture and periods of drouth, but by comparison with known records to fix the dates of such changes. Based upon cross-sections of trees now centuries old he has been able, for example, to date timbers in the early cliff dwellings, and after long research and comparison of rings has assembled a consecutive line of growth marks which can be used as a time-table. This chain of rings extending without a break from the ninth to the twentieth century is most impressive when shown on a moving film, for such evidence was not made by the hand of man. His responsibility lies in the interpretation of it and the result depends on the exactitude of the observer's measurements and calculations. Hours or days cannot be determined, but the year when a log was cut can be fixed or approximated and another instrument has been created for the archæologist to measure life before the appearance of written records.

If one should assume that the only things worth knowing about the more modern nations were their manners, customs, laws, and mechanical devices, the chronicles and written narratives would still be needed as a continuous ribbon with which to bind the other matters together. These narratives contain defects which must be sifted out. The writers may have followed too narrow a path in confining their attention to kings and wars, but at their worst they point out a line of inquiry, and at their best their work contains the necessary continuation factors of history. This is said in order that the modern historical student may neither forget nor underestimate the services of his early predecessors in an age when many new social factors demand his attention and he is told that there is a "crisis" which calls for a "new" kind of history. The call to study culture rather than kings is not so new as some have assumed. It is a pursuit by all means to be encouraged and followed, but relics without the human narrator are imperfect sources even of the history of culture. At the same time the importance of relics is very great; for the pre-literary period, indeed, they are all we have. They have been classified according to their rudeness or finish as palæolithic, neolithic, of the age of bronze, or of the age of iron. For every age or period since man began to write, his relics have been collected in museums, where Roman and medieval armor, ancient and modern jewelry, utensils of every description—all his varied inventions—are on display. All of these things reflect the culture of the people who used them, and as evidence they should be rigorously applied to the period and place where they belong. Sometimes this means a long reach of time, as in the case of the Arab plow of to-day, which is a pointed stick similar to that employed in the days of Abraham. In other cases the old gives way to an improvement, or to a totally new invention. In every instance relics are related to something else, and each must be studied in connection with its surroundings. It is a fundamental principle of archæological excavation

142

that before a find is removed from the ground notes must be taken of what lies next to it, or underneath, or in the layer above. From Schliemann's seven stages of Troy to the caves of New Mexico, relativity is everything. A recent conclusion as to the antiquity of man was based on Harrington's discovery, in a cave underneath a mass of animal dung, of the bones of a giant sloth in close proximity to charcoal remains of a camp-fire. The relics, ancient and modern, which do not need to be dug up must be handled with just as much rigorous study of their relation to other things.

The peculiar value of relics in evidence is the fact that they are unconscious witnesses. The chronicle, the extended narrative, and the biography are conscious attempts to transmit information, and however conscientious the writer may have been in his desire to tell the truth, he is liable to error or limitations of view. True, the relics have to be tested to make sure they are not fraudulent or erroneously placed, but, found genuine, they require no test of human frailty for themselves. Their silent evidence is subject only to the mistakes or fanciful interpretations of modern students, whose errors are being steadily reduced by scientific method.

As already indicated, there exists a mass of material which should be treated like arrow-head relics, although not so obviously in that class. A cuneiform tablet, a piece of parchment, or a sheet of paper of any age may contain a deed of land which originally witnessed a legal transfer of property and was of live economic value to its owner. Now its legal life has ceased and it has entered upon another vocation, also important, as a testimonial to the customs of its day. A statute of law was formed to direct the course of human conduct, and, whether in force or not, it stands as a witness of the period of its creation. So likewise with a multitude of written things which easily come to mind. A poem, a romantic tale, an advertisement, a newspaper itself, with all its conscious local history—all these are unconscious testimonials to the state of culture. For historical purposes the main duty is to distinguish and make use of the qualities which give to such relics their peculiar significance.

Analyzing still further this raw material, one encounters at certain points the transition from silence to history. To quote the same examples once more, a Celtic cromlech indicates simply a prehistoric burial; a tombstone with only a name is hardly more than a relic; but a tombstone with a date begins to be history, and still more is it history when it records the virtues and achievements of the deceased. Assyrian statuary is commonly adorned with writings which recite with no false modesty the conquests of the kings they represent, and the rest of the world has more or less followed in this path. Such relics with a double rôle are usually classified as Monuments. This class of relics may include certain kinds of public documents, where the distinction is not so plain as in the examples given above, but in all cases the visibility of a conscious effort to record events gives the signal for a different array of evidence. Even a legal writ, a preamble to a law, or a clause in a will may be infected with history, and the investigator must clearly distinguish those parts in order to give each its appropriate interpretation.

In the preceding chapters various kinds of documents have been mentioned in illustration of the topics under discussion. In making use of these materials in historical research it is most important that one should be wide awake to the class to which each belongs, for upon that depends its value as evidence and the kind of interpretation to be given it. It is not merely a question whether the written record is a relic of the time or a conscious narrative, but it is important to know from what office or jurisdiction or official it emanated in order to estimate its peculiar significance. As was said in the chapter on palæography, the understanding of a document does not depend so much on the ability to read it as on a knowledge of the administrative system under which it was issued. For English public documents Sir Hubert Hall has provided a description of the many forms stored in the Public Record Office, with a brief analysis of the functions of the various government offices. These functions are by no means fixed and stationary but have been subject to changes in their history, and consequently the duties and jurisdiction of an office must be apprehended according to the date of the document. In the study of American political history similar precaution is required. The period of time covered is only a fraction of that covered by the histories of European countries, and changes may not be so marked, but a precise knowledge of the competence and duties of any public official is necessary to a proper estimate of the documents which he issues.

Public documents of one kind or another constitute the greater part of the vast mass of material out of which history is constructed, and foremost among these are the laws under which nations or groups have lived. At various stages of civilization these have been accepted as divine proclamations, as ancestral custom, as decrees of absolute kings, as orders of kings in council, as statutes of parliaments, as voted rules of democracies. From superhuman ordinances they have developed into secular man-made regulations of conduct. From simple codes for primitive peoples they have become vast accumulations of rules which attempt to provide for the needs and emergencies of an expanded civilization. For these regulations man has assumed complete responsibility and must be given blame or credit accordingly.

A large part of the work in the field of law con-

146

sists in explanation of the reasons for the enactment of given statutes and of the process by which this end was reached. Legislative records, therefore, consist in general of two classes, namely, the statutes themselves and the records of discussion and information upon which they were based. The law will be printed in the collection of statutes, the debates over it in the journals of the houses of the legislature, and the information in the reports of the committees to which the matter was referred. Theoretically the investigator ought to be able to decide from the debates what information was accepted, but this would omit reasons and influences which appear in any legislature. Party principles, desires of constituents, and personal interest are matters not always obvious in legislative records and must be determined from other evidence. The debates will show the prominent reasons for and against, but the "swapping" of votes for other measures is not usually a matter of record. Yet, whatever may have been the action on the law, the evidence accumulated in committee reports is often highly valuable to the historian in its display of conditions in the country. Witness the importance of parliamentary reports on the labor situation in England during the first quarter of the nineteenth century, and a multitude of similar instances. The mass of this material is overwhelming, but in spite of duplications and contradictions there is much in it of economic and social importance. Here as in other cases the investigator tests the qualifications of each witness as to his ability or willingness to state the truth.

A statute is frequently preceded by a preamble giving reasons for its enactment. Such a prelude in that connection has the air of a solemn statement of fact. The assertions in the preamble may be true, but its attachment to a law is no guaranty of exactitude. These "whereas" clauses need proof in spite of the legislative endorsement, for in the last analysis they are lawmakers' excuses to be tested as conscious narrative. This need not be taken as a general indictment of the preamble, but rather as a caution to be awake to the class of historical material to which it belongs.

Reference has already been made to the limitations placed upon judicial proof as compared with evidence available to the historical investigator. These "trial rules" are products of centuries of experience in the administration of law according to the Anglo-Saxon conception of justice. While some of them are antiquated or liable to misuse, the most of these rules promote fairness in trials and are fully justifiable in view of the conditions in which litigation takes place. Let it be further said that trial rules are concerned only with the admissibility of evidence, not with its value as proof. They deal chiefly with the questions whether the testimony is worth considering or sufficiently material to the case in view of the limitations under which courts of justice must proceed.

In the first place, judicial trials must be held at a fixed time and place and a decision rendered at once. Appeals to a higher court may be made, but the conditions of trial remain the same as before. If judges and juries could take unlimited time to consider and pass judgment, great injury and hardship might be inflicted upon litigants, innocent persons might suffer, and society might be afflicted with continued crime. It is in the interest of social order that such matters be settled within a reasonable time, and usually that time is short.

Second, courts and juries have to deal with matters which have become subjects of controversy between living beings whose respective interests are at stake. Strong emotions may be evoked, and especially the eagerness to win may lead to biased statements, suppression of unfavorable parts of the truth, or downright prevarication. The temptation to fraud in various degrees is very powerful, and consequently the tribunal must prescribe the rules of procedure and admissibility of evidence which will permit it to get at the facts. The historian may in the coolness and silence of his study draw upon an unlimited variety of testimony, direct or circumstantial, from which the distractions of emotion and the danger of fraud have been practically eliminated. His topic may be a subject of controversy, but he does not anticipate that his literary adversaries will wilfully suppress the truth.

Third, that part of a court of law with which the decision of a controversy rests is composed of laymen, not scientists or experts. Juries when taken at their best are composed of intelligent citizens who have not spent a lifetime in disentangling evidence. Their common sense is relied upon to ascertain the truth, but they are assisted by rules of evidence and procedure which attempt to prevent confusion by excluding unimportant side issues and trivial data of slight value as testimony.

Fourth, the emotional conditions of a court trial are often of such a character that the evidence and arguments are likely to stir up prejudice as well as sympathy, or even contempt or ridicule. It is to prevent undue influence of such emotions upon the jury that trial rules attempt to regulate the conduct of the case so as to let the important evidence have its normal effect. Even when fraud is not present, it may be necessary in the interest of justice to control an undue exploitation of prejudicial weapons.

It is clear, therefore, that trial regulation is justified, however different the conditions may be from those of an ideal tribunal or from the advantageous position of the quiet scholar investigating the same subject. Mr. Wigmore compares these rules with the abstract science of proof and finds most of them based upon reason. Some are antiquated relics of earlier conceptions of law and should be abolished, a hope which may take time to bear fruit in view of the conservatism of courts and the legal fraternity.[1]

At the same time the study of judicial procedure offers valuable assistance to the historical investigator because of the many suggestions respecting lines of inquiry which might be overlooked. In both cases witnesses must be qualified to speak. Inferences are to be made from their origin and opportunities. Human nature, in respect to its errors of perception, vagaries of memory, and powers of narrating what has been seen, remains the same, although subject to peculiar tests in court. Consequently the analyses of testimony found in works on legal evidence are decidedly stimulating and lead to thoughtful consideration of historical proof.

In this connection we meet the question of the uses of psychology in the study of historical evidence. Great aid has been rendered by this branch of learning in the determination of motives in human action, and often upon matters of historical importance. The difference, however, between its application to evidence given in courts of law and to that found in narratives or documents deliberately written is very marked. In a judicial trial witnesses must give oral testimony under peculiar mental conditions. The surroundings, the presence of un-

[1] J. H. Wigmore, *Principles of Judicial Proof,* Appendix I.

friendly lawyers, the jury-box filled with question-marks, the confusion of cross-questioning, and many other things usually unfamiliar all produce a psychological effect upon the conscientious as well as the fraudulent witness. Even in the case of men with the best of motives the strain of public examination may affect the memory or the power to reproduce a situation. The liability to take a partial or one-sided view of what eyes have seen is already enough before going on the witness stand, and the questioning may make it worse. How well a witness comes through the ordeal is a matter of temperament, and the more sensitive are likely to suffer.

These conditions do not make it impossible for a tribunal to ascertain the essential facts in a case, but rather they help to explain contradictory testimony and the difficulties of the single witness. Psychology has done much to clarify human activity both in the individual and in the crowd. Even machines have been invented where records show when the subject is telling the truth and when he maketh a lie, but psychometry with all its marvels is a long way from the determination of the quality of evidence and as yet remains a handmaid of the judicial investigation of crime. Most of the same results can be obtained by the traditional methods of examination where counsel and court employ either instinctively or knowingly the common, everyday principles of psychology in the sense of knowledge of human nature gained from experience.

In a somewhat different way the historical student makes use of the science of the human mind. Assuming that he has before him a document or narrative the genuineness of which has been proved beyond doubt, there arise at once questions as to why the writer gave that particular form and coloration to his work. As in the case of the witness on the stand, we are obliged to determine numerous points respecting the qualifications of the author. Where he lived at the time; whether noble or peasant, priest or layman, official or plain citizen; what access he had to court life or governmental circles; and any other information will be sought to show whether or not he was qualified to observe and report on that subject. Questions as to origin, position, experience, and the like help to explain the psychological reactions of men to the circumstances which play about them and can be applied both to the writers and the actors in history.

Froissart, for example, was a courtier who had the best of opportunities to learn of the heroic deeds of his contemporaries, but we observe that the time in which he lived had its effect upon the kind of things he chose to record. It was an age when the man of war in his glittering armor was the ideal of ruling society, and Froissart not only writes with that audience in view but is so thoroughly imbued with its spirit that the lower classes, in the rare instances where they are mentioned at all, are treated with an air of contempt.

Monastic and clerical writers were more numerous in the middle ages, because the clergy were the chief depositories of learning. Some of these chroniclers were situated where they came in contact with the princes and ruling classes of their day. Their monastic houses were on the great highways, and they became conversant with political movements. By education and opportunity they were qualified to write, but it is still necessary to study their personal motives and those of their profession in order to explain the coloration of their accounts. Kings were likely to get a bad reputation if they appropriated monastic revenue, or exacted even reasonable taxation.

Examples might be quoted indefinitely to show how times have affected not only the contents of history, but the attitude of the writer toward his facts and his narrative. From an age of credulity we have progressed to an era when exactitude is demanded and largely obtained; but, whether we investigate ancient or modern history, it is absolutely necessary to determine the qualifications of every writer, even when evidently conscientious, as to ability, situation in life, opportunity for observation or inquiry, and any other matter which may affect his view of his topic. This applies with emphasis to those who narrate the events which they have witnessed or in which they have taken part, but even those who write from documents of the past are not exempt from inner and outside influences.

The ascertainment of facts is not all there is to historical study. The interpretation of these data is the end and object of the labor, and this is a task which must be renewed for every new generation of readers. In the course of time not only do new facts come to light, but new views of life and new reasons for consulting the past follow the changes in civilization. The social sciences show more and more their mutual interdependence, and new lights are reflected upon human history. Therefore the interpretation of events and actions is a serious but an exceedingly interesting occupation. The soundness of the historian's conclusions is founded on the solidity of the facts which have been ascertained.

A SELECTED BIBLIOGRAPHY

I. DEFINITION OF HISTORY

II. TESTING THE MATERIALS

General Works on Methods of Research

E. Bernheim, *Lehrbuch der historischen Methode,* 6th ed. (Leipzig, 1908). A comprehensive treatment of the materials of history, the theory of criticism, the constructive process, and the philosophy of history.

C. V. Langlois and C. Seignobos, *Introduction aux études historiques* (Paris, 1898). Translation by C. B. Berry (1898), reprinted 1912. A stimulating review of theory and practice.

C. Seignobos, *La méthode historique appliquée aux sciences sociales* (Paris, 1901).

Gustav Wolf, *Einführung in das Studium der neueren Geschichte* (Berlin, 1910). Treats of the materials of modern history and may be regarded as a complement to the work of Bernheim. Provides a bibliographical handbook of modern history, chiefly of Germany.

A. Meister, *Grundriss der Geschichtswissenschaft* (Leipzig, 1906–1917). A coöperative work by numerous authors, beginning with a brief outline of method. Practical chapters on the auxiliary sciences are cited in appropriate connection. A large part of the work consists of historiographical studies in the constitutional, economic, and religious history of Germany.

G. C. Lewis, *A Treatise on the Methods of Observation and*

Reasoning in Politics, 2 vols. (London, 1852). In spite of its age, still full of suggestion respecting the interpretation of historical materials.

E. Meyer, *Zur Theorie und Methodik der Geschichte* (Halle, 1902).

J. G. Droysen, *Grundriss der Historik,* translated by E. B. Andrews as *Outline of the Principles of History* (Boston, 1893). A compact syllabus to accompany Droysen's lectures and often quoted.

J. M. Vincent, *Historical Research; an Outline of Theory and Practice* (Henry Holt and Company, New York, 1911; reprint, P. Smith, 1929).

F. M. Fling, *The Writing of History; an Introduction to Historical Method* (New Haven, 1920).

A. L. Feder, *Lehrbuch der historischen Methodik* (Regensburg, 1919; 3d rev. ed., 1924).

B. Croce, *The Theory and Practice of History* (New York, 1921).

Allen Johnson, *The Historian and Historical Evidence* (New York, 1926).

H. W. Odum and Katharine Jocher, *Introduction to Social Research* (New York, 1929). Treats of methods, aspects in the light of various sciences, interpretation of data. The book is stimulating and suggestive.

The history of historical writing has been approached in various ways by numerous authors, from whom one may select for their scholarly treatment the following:

J. T. Shotwell, *An Introduction to the History of History* (New York, 1921).

Charles Mortet, "La science de l'histoire," in *La Grande Encyclopédie,* Vol. XX.

(Note.—Many essays by prominent historians on the nature of the study or the characteristics of a particular period can be found in their collected works or noted in bibliographical lists. These are stimulating but do not cover the field of general research.)

L. J. PAETOW, *Guide to the Study of Mediæval History,* rev. ed. (New York, 1931). Brought up to date and expanded in scope, this is the most useful handbook for the period and contains references to method and the auxiliary sciences.

Guide to Historical Literature, edited by W. H. ALLISON, S. B. FAY, A. H. SHEARER, and H. R. SHIPMAN (New York, 1931). Begun as a revision of C. K. Adams's *Manual of Historical Literature,* the work has been expanded in many directions and brought up to date of publication with the assistance of more than 350 contributors. Section A, "History and Auxiliary Sciences," 45 pages, contains the references pertinent here.

III. DIPLOMATICS

HUBERT HALL, *Studies in English Official Documents,* and *A Formula Book of English Historical Documents* (both Cambridge, 1908). Not a general treatise on diplomatics, but the best introduction to English materials.

A. MEISTER, *Grundriss der Geschichtswissenschaft,* Vol. I. In this book three authors take up separate phases by way of introduction to German diplomatics.

G. VON BELOW and F. MEINECKE, *Handbuch der mittelalterlichen und neueren Geschichte* (Munich and Berlin, 1904). The section on "Urkundenlehre" is written by three eminent experts.

H. BRESSLAU, *Handbuch der Urkundenlehre für Deutschland und Italien* (Leipzig, 1889; 2d ed., 2 vols., 1912–1915). A standard work covering all phases of the subject.

A. GIRY, *Manuel de diplomatique* (Paris, 1894; new ed., 2

vols., 1925). Based on French practice and of the highest
authority. Contains references to Anglo-Norman and English documents. Its plan of treatment is perhaps more useful to English readers than that adopted in any similar
book.

F. LEIST, *Urkundenlehre: Katechismus der Diplomatik,
Palæographie, Chronologie, und Sphragistik,* new ed.
(Leipzig, 1893). A useful short compilation of the essen-
tials of the auxiliary sciences.

IV. PALÆOGRAPHY

E. M. THOMPSON, *Handbook of Greek and Latin Palæography,* new ed. (Oxford, 1912). The best introduction to
the subject.

C. T. MARTIN, *The Record Interpreter; a Collection of Abbreviations, Latin Words and Names Used in English
Historical Manuscripts and Records,* 2d ed. (London,
1910).

C. JOHNSON and H. JENKINSON, *English Court Hand, A. D.
1066–1500* (Oxford, 1915). Illustrated chiefly from public records, with an atlas of forty-four plates.

H. JENKINSON, *Later Court Hands in England from Fifteenth to the Seventeenth Century* (Cambridge, 1927).

F. MADAN, *Books in Manuscript; a Short Introduction to
Their Study and Use,* 2d ed. (London, 1920).

M. PROU, *Manuel de paléographie,* new ed. (Paris, 1925).

B. BRETHOLTZ, "Lateinische Palaeographie," in MEISTER,
Grundriss der Geschichtswissenschaft, Band 1 (Leipzig,
1906).

S. A. TANNENBAUM, *The Handwriting of the Renaissance;
Being the Development and Characteristics of the Script of
Shakespere's Time,* with an introduction by A. H. Thorn-
dike (New York, 1930).

E. A. Lowe, "Handwriting," a chapter in *The Legacy of the Middle Ages,* edited by C. C. Crump and E. F. Jacob (Oxford, 1926).

Extensive series of facsimiles of manuscripts have been issued in the various countries of Europe. Prominent examples which illustrate the period forms of handwriting include the following:

The Palæographical Society, London. Large folio plates with examples from all periods of Western European nations.

W. Arndt and M. Tangl, *Scrifttafel zur Erlernung der lateinischen Palæographie* (Berlin, 1898–1908). More than 100 quarto plates convenient for study.

A. Chroust, *Monumenta palæographica: Denkmäler der Schriftkunst des Mittelalters,* Series I–II–III, large folio in progress (Munich and Leipzig, 1900–1933).

F. Steffens, *Lateinische Palæographie* (Berlin and Leipzig, 1929). One hundred and twenty-five plates with transcriptions and explanations of the development of Latin script.

A. Chassant, *Dictionnaire des abbréviations latines et françaises,* 5th ed. (Paris, 1884).

E. Latham, *A Dictionary of Abbreviations, Contractions, and Abbreviative Signs* (New York, 1916).

A. Cappelli, *Dizionario dei abbreviature latine ed italiene* (Milan, 1899). German translation (Leipzig, 1928).

WATERMARKS

C. M. Briquet, *Les Filigranes; dictionnaire historique des marques du papier des leur apparition vers 1282 jusqu'a 1600,* 4 vols., 4to. (Geneva, 1907).

E. Heawood, "The Use of Watermarks in Dating Old Maps and Documents," *Geographical Journal,* May, 1924. Plates with 178 examples. Based on Briquet and the author's experience.

FORGERIES IN HISTORY

Books and essays on this subject range all the way from curious literary fraud to criminal counterfeiting. From all of these the historical student may profit through a better understanding of evidence. A few examples follow from an extensive literature:

E. K. CHAMBERS, *History and Motives of Literary Forgeries* (Oxford, 1891).

H. R. MONTGOMERY, *Famous Literary Impostures* (London, 1884).

J. A. FARRER, *Literary Forgeries* (London, 1917).

T. F. TOUT, *Mediæval Forgers and Forgeries* (Manchester, 1920).

D. BLACKBURN and W. CADDELL, *The Detection of Forgery; a Practical Handbook for the Use of Bankers, Solicitors, Magistrates, Clerks, and All Handling Suspected Documents* (London, 1909).

A. S. OSBURN, *Questioned Documents* (Rochester, 1910). Analysis of doubtful materials and methods of testing for genuineness.

————————, *The Problem of Proof, Especially as Exemplified in Disputed Document Trials* (New York, 1922). Contains an extensive bibliography on evidence.

V. CHRONOLOGY

Books of dates abound without number and are useful assistants to the memory. It should be remembered, however, that these lists are not proofs of dates. When questioned, the facts must be obtained through the processes of diplomatics or chronology.

L'Art de vérifier les dates is a huge compilation of tables of events with dates established by the best authority available, and finally published in forty-four volumes (Paris, 1818–1844).

MAS LATRIE, *Trésor de chronologie, d'histoire et de géographie* (Paris, 1889). A folio volume following the same plan. A modern expert declares both unreliable and warns us that great care should be exercised in using the older compilers of dates.

H. GROTEFEND, *Zeitrechnung des deutschen Mittelalters und der Neuzeit,* 2 vols. (Hannover, 1891–1898). A work of greatest value to historical students. Grotefend published later a shorter *Taschenbuch der Zeitrechnung des deutschen Mittelalters und der Neuzeit* (3rd ed., Hannover, 1910) and also a chapter on chronology in MEISTER, *Grundriss der Geschichtswissenschaft.*

For English history valuable aid will be found in:

J. J. BOND, *Handy Book of Rules and Tables for Verifying Dates,* 4th ed. (London, 1889).

E. A. FRY, *Almanacks for Students of English History* (London, 1915). Very convenient because the arrangement obviates the necessity of consulting numerous tables for one problem.

H. FITCH, *The Perfect Calendar for every Year of the Christian Era.* 8 vo. 45 pp. (N. Y. and London, 1927).

R. L. POOLE, *The Beginning of the Year in the Middle Ages* (Oxford, 1921).

VI. THE SEAL

Scholarly chapters on the subject of seals will be found in the general works on diplomatics. See GIRY, *Manuel de diplomatique,* Chapter IX; BRESSLAU, *Handbuch der Diplomatik,* Vol. I, chapter on "Die Besiegelung"; MEISTER, *Grundriss der Geschichtswissenschaft,* section by TH. ILGEN on "Sphragistik"; *Grande Encyclopédie,* under "Sigillographie," with extensive bibliography.

VII. HERALDRY

Although the various countries of Europe have shown different tastes in the artistic display of armorial bearings, the underlying theory is the same for all of them and the technical terms used are practically identical. Consequently an English work provides a satisfactory introduction to the general subject.

J. WOODWARD and G. BURNETT, *A Treatise on Heraldry, British and Foreign,* 2 vols. (Edinburgh, 1892; new ed., 1896).

FRANCIS J. GRANT, *Manual of Heraldry,* new rev. ed. (London, 1924).

A. C. FOX-DAVIES, *A Complete Guide to Heraldry,* rev. ed. (London, 1925).

All of the above are copiously illustrated and provided with glossaries of terms.

For tracing specific coats of arms the great work for Germany is SIEBMACHER's *Wappenbuch,* which in the course of the three centuries of its publication has accumulated a mass of data and illustrations until it fills some 483 folio parts.

D'HOZIER, *Armorial général de la France,* 14 vols., performs a similar service. ERICH GRITZNER, "Heraldik," a section in MEISSNER, *Grundriss der Geschichtswissenschaft,* shows the application of heraldry in historical research.

VIII. WEIGHTS, MEASURES, AND MONEY

Early methods of calculation are explained in various histories of mathematics, of which the two below provide satisfactory accounts in plain language. English practice, early and late, will be found in Recorde, Hall, and Barnard.

F. CAJORI, *History of Mathematics,* 2d ed. (New York, 1919).

D. E. SMITH, *History of Mathematics,* 2 vols. (New York, 1923).

ROBERT RECORDE, *The Ground of Artes* (first printed in 1542; later editions numerous). Edition of 1610 has the title "The Ground of Artes, etc. whereunto are also added divers tables by John Mellis, and now lastly corrected by John Wade. London, printed for John Harrison dwelling on Paternoster Row at the figure of the Greyhound" (copy in the Huntington Library).

HUBERT HALL, *The Red Book of the Exchequer,* Rolls Series (London, 1896).

F. P. BARNARD, and H. W. C. DAVIS, *Mediæval England, a New Edition of Barnard's Companion to English History* (Oxford and New York, 1924). Bibliography.

F. P. BARNARD, *The Casting Counter and the Counting Board* (London, 1916).

Encyclopædia Britannica, article "Abacus."

HUBERT HALL and J. NICHOLAS FRIED, editors, *Select Tracts and Table Books Relating to English Weights and Measures* (1100–1742), Camden Miscellany, Vol. XV;

General Series, Vol. XLI (1929). Bibliography and index of metrological terms.

S. LANE POOLE, *Coins and Medals; Their Place in History and Art,* 3d ed. (London, 1894). Contains also illuminating data of genealogical and biographical value.

G. F. HILL, *Coins and Medals,* Helps for Students of History, No. 36 (London, 1920).

——————, *Historical Greek Coins* (London, 1906).

——————, *Historical Roman Coins* (London, 1909).

G. MACDONALD, *Coin Types; Their Origin and Development* (Glasgow, 1905).

IX. GENEALOGY

Books on genealogy approach the subject in various ways. Compilations showing the descent of sovereigns and important families are numerous and helpful. Of histories of families, both conspicuous and otherwise, there is an untold multitude in single volumes and heavy compendiums. Usually these give little more than relationships, and hence further particulars of the lives of members of a family must be sought in dictionaries of biography when the person is sufficiently important. Guides to research in family history point out many of the sources to be examined and are decidedly useful to the general historian as well. Finally a few writers have attacked the problems of heredity. The *Encyclopædia Britannica* under "Genealogy" provides an extensive bibliography and a paragraph of solid advice to investigators in that field. Rye's *Records* is an excellent introduction to the many forms of documents which must be consulted. The theory of the subject is traversed in Lorenz, Galton, Woods, and Heydenreich.

H. B. GEORGE, *Genealogical Tables Illustrative of European History,* 5th ed. revised (Oxford, 1916).

A. M. H. J. Stokvis, *Manuel d'histoire de généalogie et de chronologie de tous les états du globe,* 3 vols. (Leyden, 1888–1891).

O. Lorenz, *Lehrbuch der gesammten wissenschaftlichen Genealogie* (Berlin, 1898).

Francis Galton, *Natural Inheritance* (New York, 1889).

————————, "Hereditary Genius" (extract from the foregoing), in Warner's Library of the World's Best Literature, Vol. XI.

F. A. Woods, *Mental and Moral Heredity in Royalty; a Statistical Study in History and Psychology,* 104 portraits (New York, 1906).

W. Rye, *Records and Record Searching; a Guide to the Genealogist and Topographer,* 2d ed. (London, 1897).

G. W. Marshall, *The Genealogist's Guide* (London, 1879; 4th ed., Guilford, 1903).

J. H. Lea, *Genealogical Research in England, Scotland and Ireland; a Handbook for the Student* (Boston, 1906).

Library of Congress, *American and English Genealogies in the Library,* 2d ed., by M. A. Gilkey (Washington, 1919). References to nearly 7,000 titles of books.

Eduard K. H. Heydenreich, *Handbuch der praktischen Genealogie,* 2 vols. (Leipzig, 1913). Treats of the theory of family history, with systematic discussion of every class of pertinent materials. Valuable alike to the genealogist and the general student of history.

X. DIPLOMACY

E. Satow, *A Guide to Diplomatic Practice,* 2 vols., 2d ed. (London and New York, 1922). An indispensable manual for persons entering the diplomatic service.

J. W. Foster, *The Practice of Diplomacy as Illustrated in the Foreign Relations of the United States* (Boston and

New York, 1906). The author states that it is "not a manual of diplomatic procedure," but intended to show what Americans have done to improve the service, and by means of such a popular narrative to indicate the rules of diplomatic procedure. Bibliography.

C. DE MARTENS, *Guide diplomatique,* new rev. ed. (Leipzig, 1866).

F. PRADIER-FODÉRÉ, *Cours de droit diplomatique* (Paris, 1881).

Embajada Espanola; an Anonymous Contemporary Spanish Guide to Diplomatic Procedure in the Last Quarter of the Seventeenth Century, translated and edited by the Rev. H. J. Chaytor, Camden Miscellany, Vol. XIV; Third Series, Vol. XXXVII (London, 1926). An interesting picture of old-fashioned ideas of diplomacy.

XI. GEOGRAPHY

J. K. WRIGHT, *Aids to Geographical Research; Bibliographies and Periodicals* (American Geographical Society, New York, 1923).

H. B. GEORGE, *The Relations of Geography and History,* 5th rev. ed., edited by Howarth and Fawcett (Oxford, 1924).

ISAAC TAYLOR, *Names and Their Histories* (London, 1896; rev. ed., London, 1898).

F. J. TURNER, *Report of a Committee of the American Historical Association on the Relations of Geography to History,* Annual Report of the American Historical Association, 1907, Vol. I.

A. RATZEL, *Anthropogeographie,* 2 vols. (1882–1891, 4th ed. of Vol. I, Stuttgart, 1921; 2d ed. of Vol. II, 1912).

ELLEN C. SEMPLE, *Influences of Geographic Environment,*

on the Basis of Ratzel's System of Anthropogeography (New York and London, 1911).

RAY H. WHITBECK and OLIVE J. THOMAS, *The Geographic Factor; Its Rôle in Life and Civilization* (New York, 1932).

P. VIDAL DE LA BLACHE, *Principles of Human Geography,* edited by Emmanuel de Martonne, translated from the French by Millicent Todd Bingham (New York, 1926).

P. VIDAL DE LA BLACHE and L. GALLOIS, editors, *Géographie Universelle* (Paris, 1927 etc.).

ELLSWORTH HUNTINGTON and S. M. CUSHING, *Principles of Human Geography* (1920; 3d rev. ed., New York, 1924, London, 1925).

ELLSWORTH HUNTINGTON, *Civilization and Climate* (3d. rev. ed., New Haven, 1924, London, 1925).

WALTER P. WEBB, *The Great Plains* (Boston, 1931). A study of human geography applied to a specific environment.

M. I. NEWBIGIN, *Geographical Aspects of Balkan Problems in Their Relation to the Great European War* (London and New York, 1915).

——————————, *Frequented Ways; a General Survey of Land Forms, Climate and Vegetation of Western Europe, Considered in Their Relation to the Life of Man, Including a Detailed Study of Some Typical Regions* (London and Boston, 1922).

DOUGLAS W. JOHNSON, *Topography and Strategy in the War* (New York, 1917).

XII. HISTORICAL EVIDENCE

ALLEN JOHNSON, *The Historian and Historical Evidence* (New York, 1926).

J. H. WIGMORE, *The Principles of Judicial Proof as Given*

by Logic, Psychology and General Experience and Illustrated in Judicial Trials (Boston, 1913; 2d edition revised, 1931).

JAMES SCHOULER, *Historical Testimony,* Reports of American Historical Association, 1895.

J. B. THAYER, *A Treatise on the Law of Evidence at the Common Law* (Boston, 1898).

INDEX

172

(1)